From EdTech to PedTech

Aimed at teachers and leaders looking to create greater impact on teaching and learning through the use of digital technology in schools, *From EdTech to PedTech* translates research on the effective integration of digital technology in education into relevant, accessible, and practical guidance for teachers and school leaders. This much-needed handbook bridges the gap between knowing 'what works' and knowing how to make it work for you and your learners.

Bringing much-needed precision, fresh insights and clarity to the thinking, planning, and the integration of digital technology in teaching and learning, this practical handbook:

- guides practitioners through 'must know' research findings and what they mean for everyday practice
- unpacks different ideas about pedagogy and how these inform digital technology use
- introduces the Funnels of Influence model to help you understand why you think and do the things that you do
- provides practical self-audit tools that can be used individually and across teams to clearly identify pedagogical priorities
- provides structured audit and review tools to ensure that strategies are based on sound research and result in practical, impactful, actions
- provides teachers with practical guidance to ensure that precision planning and a clear focus on impact lead to lasting and meaningful teaching and learning experiences for all learners.

This engaging research-informed guide is an essential resource for any school leader or classroom teacher looking to maximise the value and the learning impact of digital technology in their school.

Fiona Aubrey-Smith is an award-winning teacher and leader, Director of One Life Learning, Founder of PedTech, Associate Lecturer and Consultant Researcher at The Open University, and Founding Fellow of the Chartered College of Teaching. She was named in 2022 as one of the 50 most influential people in education.

Peter Twining is Professor of Education (Innovation in Schooling and Educational Technology) at the University of Newcastle (Australia). He has been a primary school teacher, Professor of Education and Head of Department of Education at the Open University (UK), the Co-Director of the Centre for Research in Education and Educational Technology, and Co-Editor in Chief of *Computers & Education*.

"It is way over time to rethink educational technology. This is a brilliant book about such rethinking of digital technology in education."

Professor Yong Zhao, Foundation Distinguished Professor, University of Kansas and Professor in Educational Leadership, Melbourne Graduate School of Education

"This book goes to the heart of embracing digital technology as a resource to support pedagogical practice. Interactive elements encourage deep reflection about teaching intent, ensuring that professional self-knowledge about pedagogical style and belief is aligned with the ways in which digital learning is designed. Through understanding and knowing yourself as a teacher the opportunities for digital innovation become crystal clear. A must-have resource for anyone aiming to become a champion of technology that can transform learning."

Professor Dame Alison Peacock, Chief Executive, Chartered College of Teaching

"As an educator, one of the most powerful things you can do is to align our pedagogical beliefs and practices with the effective use of technology in the classroom. And that's exactly what Fiona and Peter's book provides – a road map for teachers to invest in their own professional capital and improve the life chances of children in their care. A must-read for those committed to driving change and taking their own practice to the next level."

Karine George, Chief Education Officer, Educate, and former Headteacher

"Like it or not, and still many teachers don't much like it, the future of teaching is going to be far more technology driven. Read this book, and it will ensure that the technology will be used in the interests of students and genuine imaginative learning."

Sir Anthony Seldon, Emeritus Professor and former Vice Chancellor of the University of Buckingham

"We have been waiting for something like this that bridges the gap between pedagogy and technology. For too long they have been seen by many as mutually exclusive. This book will greatly support every teacher's learning – a must for every school."

Claire Lowe, CEO, The Inspire Learning Partnership and member of the Department for Education Headteacher Advisory Board

"The 50 year EdTech revolution has consistently over-promised and under-delivered. Here, Fiona and Peter explore the missing links, and in PedTech they build the foundation all educators should reference before they invest if they want significant return."

Stephen Cox, Founder, World Education Summit, Chief Executive, Osiris Educational

"For decades, books have implored teachers to use EdTech with not a lot of success. Covid fixed that problem. Now to capitalise on this usage, and not watch the slip back into the old grammar of schooling, Aubrey-Smith and Twining highlight the "why" – the importance of understanding teacher beliefs. This book introduces the Funnel of Influences and the pivotal role of pedagogical alignment – a powerful notion. It's well worth reading this book to better and deeper understand these concepts."

"Who's driving the EdTech bus? After reading this book, you will become the driver."

Professor John Hattie, Emeritus Professor, Melbourne Graduate School of Education and Chair of the Board of the Australian Institute for Teaching and School Leadership

"In the earliest days of EdTech the steady stream of remarkable new technologies suggested a future full of excitingly effective new directions for learners and learning: multimedia, high-capacity storage, digital video, natural language programming, portable and pocketable devices, the World Wide Web code, trouble-free communications, rich data, and so much more. Disappointingly the heroic teachers and children who danced with delight at these myriad opportunities were let down by the rather dull policies and pedagogies that resulted. Why?"

"But then along comes this excellent, timely, book which not only tackles the "why?!" but also nourishes the souls of those heroic pioneers by re-arming them with pragmatism, awareness, clarity, and esteem. Hurrah to all that."

Professor Stephen Heppell, Felipe Segovia Chair in Learning Innovation at Universidad Camilo José Cela, Madrid

"It's lovely to read a book that states boldly at the outset that human beings are at the heart of education. A book that uses the word pedagogy and explains what it means. This is a great read full of practical advice and useful information for any teacher, parent or learner who wants to get the best from EdTech."

Professor Rose Luckin, Founder and Director of Educate and Professor of Learner Centred Design, UCL Knowledge Lab

"From EdTech to PedTech has arrived at exactly the right time. The pandemic driven rush to embrace digital technologies has by now given way to more evenly paced considerations. Should schools return to pre-pandemic approaches to technology or reset and accept that technology has irreversibly changed our lives? As Aubrey-Smith and Twining rightly point out, the pandemic may have brought these discussions to life but the dilemma upon which they are premised has been around since the first computer entered the first school."

"Schools are so caught up with the need to perform according to whatever policy matrix they are being judged by at any given time, they do not always get the time to consider the beliefs, philosophies, ideas or desirable outcomes that sit. They might not even see it as necessary."

"In leading us away from EdTech towards PedTech, the central premise of the book, Aubrey-Smith and Twining offer more than return or reset. They inspire renew. With a careful and detailed explication of why alignment between pedagogical beliefs, intentions and practice matters, the authors offer a series of activities designed to change pedagogic practice to the benefit of our pupils."

"It is a great book. Nicely written, accessible without over simplification, and practical. Designed to get teachers thinking."

Dr Carol Azumah Dennis, Deputy Associate Dean, The Open University

"This book encourages teachers to consider how they use technology and how this aligns with their pedagogical beliefs. This deep-level focus on the "why", rather than just the "what", of edtech, is exactly what we need in education to ensure that where technology is used, it really adds value to pupils' learning. I congratulate Fiona Aubrey-Smith and Peter Twining on this very important book."

Emma Goto, Senior Lecturer in Primary Education, University of Winchester

"A thought-provoking perspective on how to better integrate technology in education to achieve meaningful learning outcomes. Delving into the complexities of the current discourse on EdTech, this book argues for a change to the way we think about digital technology in pedagogically led practice, moving from the ideology of EdTech to PedTech. This is a must-read for educators and educational leaders who want to stay ahead of the curve in the ever-evolving world of technology and education."

Dr Neelam Parmar, Director of Digital Learning, Asia International School and Chief Digital Officer for E-ACT

"For a long while now, we have been told that technology will change the way we learn. This book points out that, until we adapt pedagogy to embrace the potential of technology, the promise will remain unfulfilled. More than that, the book explains how pedagogy can unleash the potential we have anticipated for so long. Read it and act!"

Professor Mick Waters, Wolverhampton University, and former Director of Curriculum for the Qualifications and Curriculum Authority

"It is beyond refutation that investments in digital technology for schools have yet to live up to the hyperbole. As Fiona and Peter eloquently assert, focusing on aligning foundational pedagogies with the use of digital tools provides a much-need balance to the spectre of technological determinism which currently dominates the global narrative."

Dr Sonny Magana, Chief Educational Optimist, Magana Education

"I couldn't stop reading it! It is so good to see a practical application from cover to cover. Dr. Aubrey-Smith and Prof. Twining present a step-by-step framework for self-reflection on our pedagogical practices, intentions, and beliefs. This framework allows teachers to focus on their expertise while using technology to augment learning possibilities. I loved the personas with different teaching and learning styles, as it connects theory to practice for better clarity to the reader. In a world where artificial intelligence is gaining terrain, this book is timely to guide education systems in their journey to answer the demands of the fourth industrial revolution. I truly enjoyed reading it!"

Erika Twani, Co-Founder and CEO, Learning One-to-One Foundation

"This book manages something that is unusual in the world of education; it appeals to those who are great advocates of technology and all that it offers, as well as those who are a little more sceptical. It does this by offering a laser-sharp focus on the effective pedagogy that must underpin the successful use of any technology. As a long-time advocate for the need to ensure technology use in schools is not simply a case of leaping on the next shiny device, the book is a breath of fresh air. Its format, too, makes it something special; it moves seamlessly from a detailed and intelligent consideration of what research says around education technology to reflective activities, examples and case studies that give real opportunity to support and change practice."

Cat Scutt MBE, Director of Education and Research, Chartered College of Teaching

"Here is the best attempt I've seen to think through the implications of the accelerating changes in educational technologies for everyday teaching - the challenges teachers face and the practical ways in which they can turn them into opportunities. It should be read by every school who will want a copy in their staff library and use it as a cornucopia of ideas for continuing professional development."

Professor Sir Tim Brighouse, Former Schools Commissioner, Leader of London Challenge, Visiting Professor at the Institute of Education, UCL

"If you have ever thought that some EdTech enthusiasts are stoking the hype cycle; then this is the book for you. Grounded in pedagogy, this book explores fertile ground - EdTech is a powerful tool to support teaching and learning. It's the pedagogy - the thinking - that makes the tool work. This book is an important moment for our EdTech movement. Imagine, a teaching profession supported properly by technology and their pedagogies supported by EdTech. Over claims have done us all a disservice and this timely and powerful book corrects the course."

Ty Goddard, Founder of The Education Foundation, Chair of EdTechUK

"What a unique book, providing a unique perspective on EdTech – considering digital technology in education through the lens of effective pedagogy. This well researched book is highly practical, thought-provoking and essential reading in the post pandemic world of EdTech. This book will guide you, whether you consider yourself to be an EdTech novice or expert."

Bukky Yusuf, Senior Leader, Leadership Development Coach & Education Consultant

"This book is about EdTech in practice and explores the relationship between pedagogical beliefs, intentions, and practices. It sets out six key messages about EdTech and clarifies research terminology and approaches. The book takes the reader on a journey through four different pedagogical belief systems, introduces the Funnel of Influences model, and provides key terminology to support thinking more precisely about pedagogical practice. It explores how digital technology can be used in different ways depending on the teacher's pedagogical beliefs and highlights the importance of precision planning. The book encourages the reader to reflect on their beliefs and practices and to bring greater alignment between their beliefs, intentions, and actions. The provocations in the book are intended to move the reader beyond their comfort zone and to see that they have more control over their future pedagogical practices than they might have realized."

ChatGPT!

From EdTech to PedTech

Changing the Way We Think about Digital Technology

Fiona Aubrey-Smith and Peter Twining

LONDON AND NEW YORK

Designed cover image: © Getty Images

First published 2024
by Routledge
4 Park Square, Milton Park, Abingdon, Oxon, OX14 4RN

and by Routledge
605 Third Avenue, New York, NY 10158

Routledge is an imprint of the Taylor & Francis Group, an informa business

British Library Cataloguing-in-Publication Data
A catalogue record for this book is available from the British Library

Library of Congress Cataloging-in-Publication Data
Names: Aubrey-Smith, Fiona, 1980- author. | Twining, P. (Peter), Professor, author.
Title: From EdTech to PedTech : changing the way we think about digital technology / Fiona Aubrey-Smith & Peter Twining.
Description: Abingdon, Oxon ; New York, NY : Routledge, 2024. | Includes bibliographical references and index.
Identifiers: LCCN 2023012473 (print) | LCCN 2023012474 (ebook) | ISBN 9781032343488 (hardback) | ISBN 9781032343495 (paperback) | ISBN 9781003321637 (ebook)
Subjects: LCSH: Computer-assisted instruction--Planning. | Educational technology--Planning.
Classification: LCC LB1028.5 .A77 2024 (print) | LCC LB1028.5 (ebook) | DDC 371.33/44678--dc23/eng/20230517
LC record available at https://lccn.loc.gov/2023012473
LC ebook record available at https://lccn.loc.gov/2023012474

ISBN: 978-1-032-34348-8 (hbk)
ISBN: 978-1-032-34349-5 (pbk)
ISBN: 978-1-003-32163-7 (ebk)

DOI: 10.4324/9781003321637

Typeset in Bembo
by SPi Technologies India Pvt Ltd (Straive)

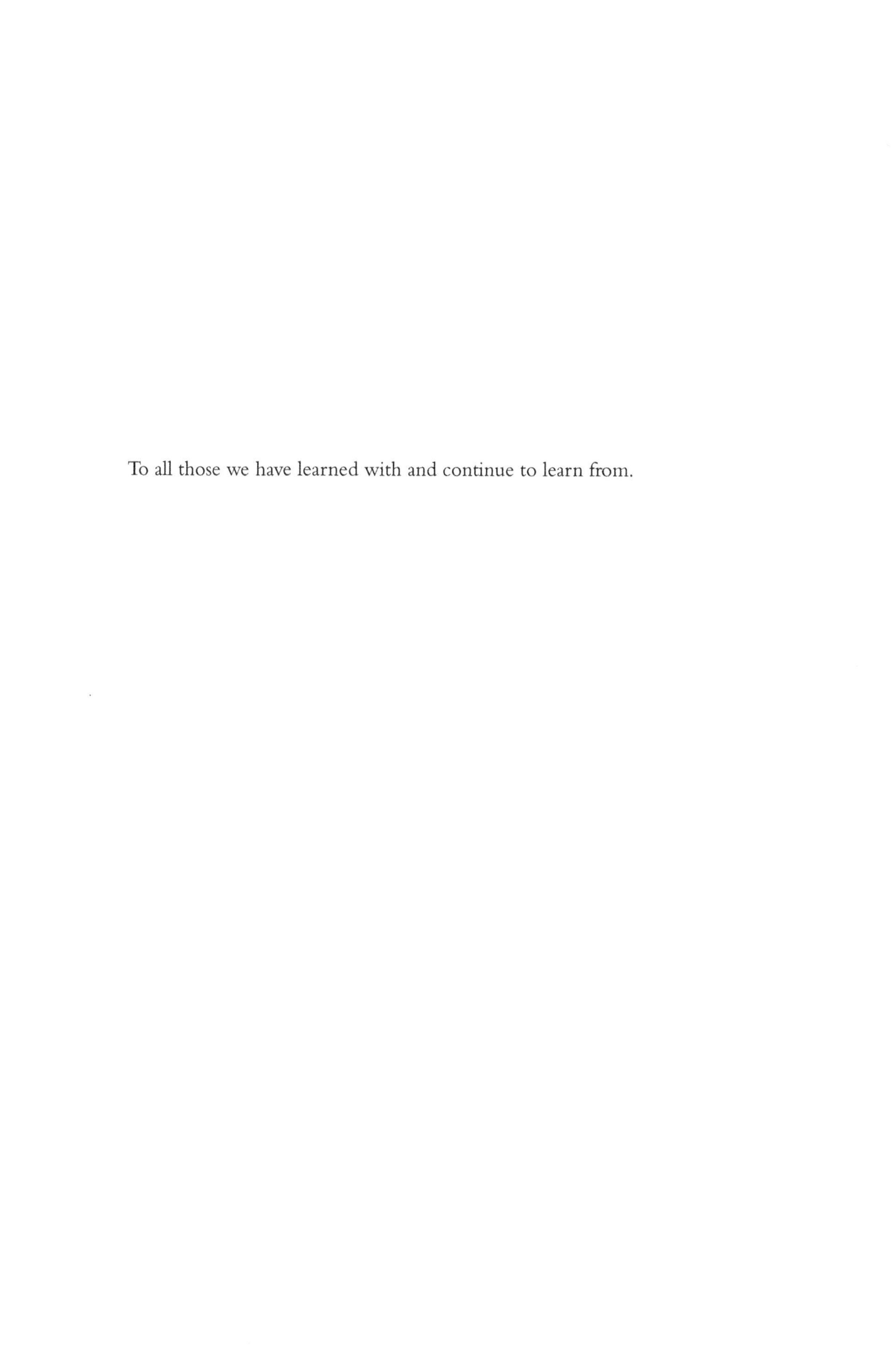

To all those we have learned with and continue to learn from.

Contents

Illustrations

Figures

Tables

Professional Learning Activities

You can download an editable and printable document version of all Guided Activities and Team Development Activities from www.onelifelearning.co.uk/resources

About the Authors

Dr Fiona Aubrey-Smith EdD MA(Ed) MMus PGCE BA(Hons) FCCT FRSA FHEA

Named by Education Business as one of the 50 most influential people in education (2022), Dr Fiona Aubrey-Smith is an award-winning teacher and leader with a passion for supporting those who work with children and young people. As the director of One Life Learning and the founder of PedTech, Fiona provides strategic education consultancy services to schools and trusts, professional learning providers, and EdTech companies. She is also an associate lecturer at The Open University, a founding fellow of the Chartered College of Teaching, and sits on the board of a number of multi-academy and charitable trusts. Fiona also writes regular articles and columns for a number of education publications and is a regular contributor to books, panels, and papers about education, pedagogy, and education technology.

@FionaAS

https://www.linkedin.com/in/fionaaubreysmith/

Professor Peter Twining PhD PGCE BA(Hons)

As an international thought leader, Professor Peter Twining is passionate about enhancing education systems at scale, with a glowing record of high-level success following in his wake. He is Professor of Education (Innovation in Schooling & Educational Technology) at the University of Newcastle, Australia, he has formerly been Head of the Department of Education at The Open University and Co-Director of the Centre for Research in Education and Educational Technology. He has also been on the Council of the British Educational Research Association, Co-Editor in Chief of *Computers & Education* (the leading journal in the field), and an editorial board member of multiple international journals and has won numerous accolades and awards for his work. Armed with his significant expertise in learning, pedagogy and digital technology, Peter is focused on the purposes of education, the management of educational change, and enhancing education systems.

@PeterT

https://www.linkedin.com/in/peter-twining/

Preface

In writing this book, we have drawn on thousands of hours of research, leadership, consulting, and teaching and from working with schools, policy shapers, and industry and academic partners. We have brought together the findings, ideas, struggles, and solutions that have faced many thousands of classroom teachers, school leaders, system leaders, researchers, politicians, and industry partners.

The thread that runs throughout this book is a commitment to championing a greater focus on learners themselves. There is an unintentional habit that we all have of conceptualising learners only as parts of an organisation (e.g. 'this cohort' or learners in 'our school'). We know (but often forget in practice) that any individual learner brings a life story into our classroom and leaves us on a trajectory that transcends our organisation. Our call to action – in whatever role we play – is to more explicitly draw this knowledge into our thinking and decision-making.

We approach this book from a particular perspective (aligned with Sociocultural theory), whereby learners and learning are socially situated and each of us – as human beings – is a unique combination of all that has come before us. However, it is important – both to us and to the wider educational field – to recognise that many perspectives exist within education. Similarly, whilst our backgrounds are situated within the Global North, our key messages are globally applicable. We have designed the content and approach of this book to prompt an open dialogue about a diverse range of pedagogical perspectives – not just those that we personally align with. Furthermore, whilst our focus and examples relate to school-aged learners, the core messages – about learning – are arguably applicable across all ages and contexts.

At its heart, this book invites, encourages, and champions a more precise and forensic conversation about supporting learning, using digital technology where that is the most effective approach.

We hope that this book will enhance practice and stimulate debate, and we look forward to your feedback.

Contact the authors at PedTech@OneLifeLearning.co.uk

Acknowledgement

We would like to acknowledge Prof. Patricia Murphy, whose expertise, professional support, and Innovative Pedagogy Framework (see https://halfbaked.education/murphys-innovative-pedagogy-framework/) have underpinned our own understanding of pedagogical stances.

Any errors of interpretation are entirely our own.

CHAPTER

1

Introduction

Why this book, and why now?

You have started to read this book because you have an interest in Educational Technologies (EdTech). You are curious about the title – encouraging readers to shift from thinking about EdTech to thinking about Pedagogically led uses of Technology (PedTech). You might be wondering why PedTech is any different to EdTech or why any kind of change in thinking is necessary. Or you might already be familiar with this conversation and be keen to hear more about what is being said. Whatever your background and whatever your perspective, we welcome you. Importantly, we also want to thank you for being part of what is now a global conversation involving practitioners, researchers, industry players and policymakers.

As you read these words – whether online, through audio or as printed pages – you will not be surprised that EdTech currently represents about 5% of the global education expenditure – a staggering US$6.5 trillion in 2022 (Holon, 2022). Furthermore, you are unlikely to be surprised that the sudden worldwide investment in technology made as a result of the coronavirus pandemic is considered by economists and analysts to be part of a wider increasing trend and reflective of a continued priority for future investment in education (Cooper Gibson, 2021). You will already be aware that the majority of schools (and organisations that work with schools) are investing strategically in ways to improve teaching and learning through the use of digital technology.

Yet there remain some sources of great friction when we talk about EdTech.

First, it seems clear that digital technology has seen more investment than impact. There is a significant reality–rhetoric gap which continues to this day in which

> there is a repetitive cycle of technology in education that goes through hype, investment, poor integration, and lack of educational outcomes. The cycle keeps spinning only because each new technology re-initiates the cycle.
>
> *(Kasinathan, 2021 p. 25)*

DOI: 10.4324/9781003321637-1

Second, there has been a tendency to focus on the technology itself rather than concentrating on the needs of learners, which Kasinathan (2021, p.21) describes as a "hammer looking for a nail". This is despite the fact that over the last 30-plus years, there have been repeated calls for the focus to be on educational needs (e.g. Rhodes, 1989; Robinson, 1993), the ways in which technology is being used (e.g. Squires & McDougall, 1994; Twining, 2002) and the need to focus on pedagogical issues (e.g. Maddux & Waggoner, 1993; Cloke, 2000; Aubrey-Smith, 2021). This idea is not new.

The friction in conversation about EdTech is therefore largely a result of the irony that we are still immersed in that same conversation today (e.g. Vicentini et al., 2022). For example, the Education Endowment Foundation (EEF) published a report synthesising existing literature about using digital technology to improve learning in 2019, which stated this key finding:

> technology must be used in a way that is informed by effective pedagogy.
>
> *(EEF, 2019, p. 3)*

However, we must be mindful that sometimes the use of digital technology can *prevent* effective learning. For example, the Organisation for Economic Co-operation and Development runs an international teaching and learning survey of teachers (TALIS) which found that the

> [i]nadequate use of digital technology is a hindrance to quality instruction.
>
> *(TALIS, 2018 p. 23)*

Yet research about the use of digital technology in education consistently tells us that it is not technology itself that has an impact on learning but the way in which digital technology is used (Luckin et al., 2018).

For those with an interest in Educational Technology, the frustrations of this inertia have been keenly felt and many have sought to be catalysts for change (e.g. Buchanan, 2020; Selwyn & Facer, 2021; Selwyn, 2018), for example by championing specialist support agencies, working parties, increased funding and policy change. There are also often calls for further research, although the evidence suggests that the problem is not a lack of understanding of the issues but a lack of the will to implement the widely acknowledged solutions (Twining, 2019).

We argue for an alternative and perhaps simpler solution: a change to the way that we think about digital technology – moving from EdTech to PedTech.

When we talk about EdTech, we are often focusing our attention on education systems and Pedagogical Practices. These are things that are observable and can be trained and then replicated: classroom techniques, timetabling and assessment processes, security and safety. An EdTech lens considers the Curriculum (what needs to be learnt), Assessment (what has been learnt and how good the educational provision is), and Pedagogical Approaches (e.g. teaching reading through synthetic phonics). Digital technology is seen as a tool to support each of those elements.

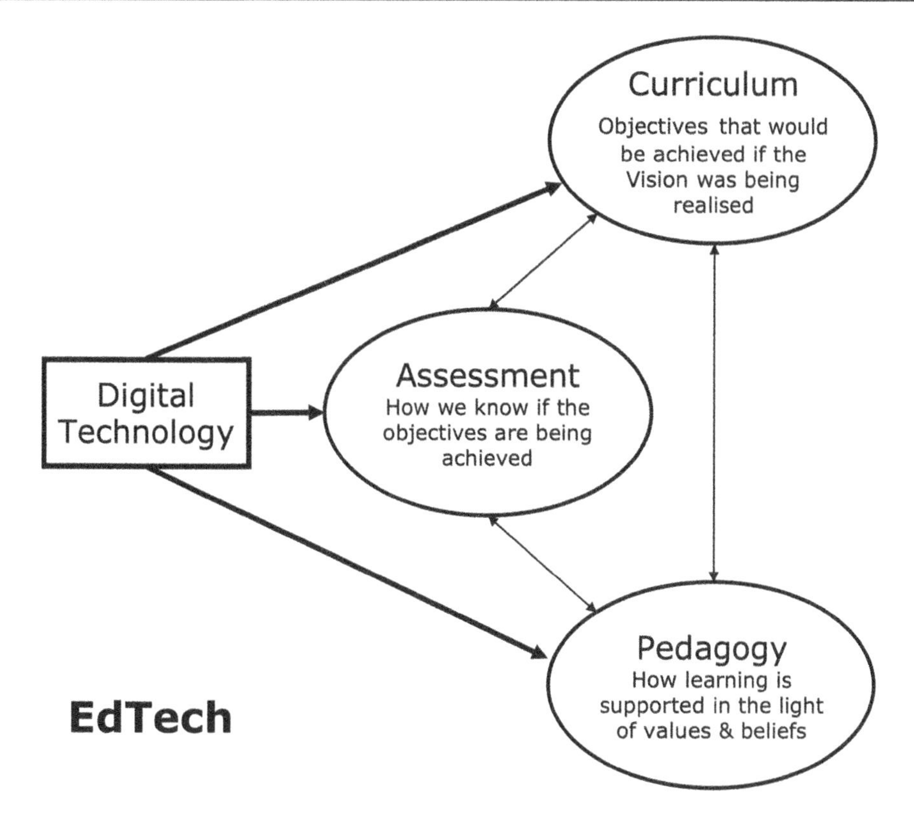

Figure 1.1 An EdTech-framed model of thinking about digital technology

However, an EdTech framing ignores important aspects of a bigger picture.

Any kind of education is driven by a purpose or vision which is informed by values and beliefs – both individually and collectively. The consequent curriculum sets out what would be being learnt if that vision were being achieved. Assessment provides evidence about the extent to which the curriculum is being achieved, and hence, the vision is being realised. Pedagogy is based on values and beliefs, including about how, why, and when people learn.

A PedTech framed model (Figure 1.2) recognises that assessment drives practice in education by modifying the curriculum and pedagogy. Digital technology is seen as being central, because it impacts so many elements within the model.

What we need to remember is that at the heart of education are human beings – learners, teachers, leaders, families – each of whom interacts through different kinds of relationships and behaviours, which are informed by different values and beliefs.

Pedagogy, which we explain more fully in Chapter 4, includes Pedagogical Practices which are underpinned by values and beliefs (your Pedagogical Stance). So our argument is that digital technology use should be viewed through the lens of values and beliefs (your Pedagogical Stance). If we want to see digital technology make a greater impact on learning, then we need that mindset shift, from

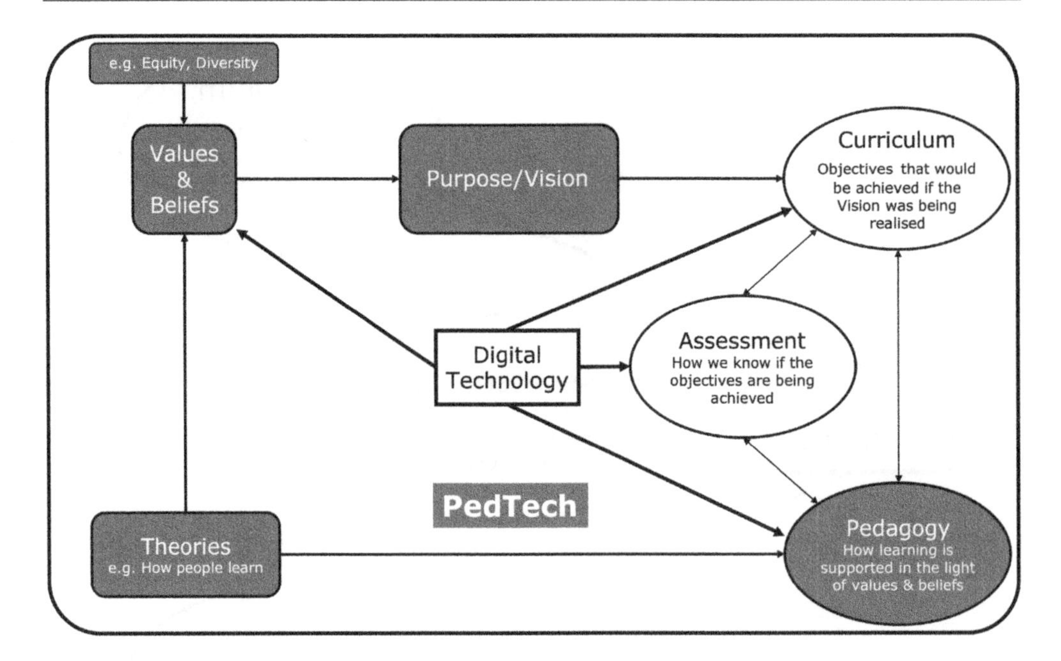

Figure 1.2 A PedTech framed model for thinking about digital technology

EdTech to PedTech – not least to catalyse the right kinds of conversations across the profession.

Our focus in this book is on the interactions between digital technology and pedagogy, but it is critical to note that these represent a small part of the overall system and that sustained change in education is unlikely to happen unless all elements of that system are aligned (Butler et al., 2018). Many have written about other elements – infrastructure, networks, devices and connectivity (e.g. Rodriguez et al., 2022), management information systems and eSafety (e.g. UKCIS, 2020) and digital skills and digital literacy (e.g. Kemp & Berry, 2019; Royal Society, 2017), to name but a few. Our focus is on the relationship between pedagogy and digital technology.

In Chapter 2, we set out six key messages that you need to know about EdTech in practice – drawing on international theoretical and empirical research and professional practice. We also clarify research terminology and approaches, highlighting some of the embedded issues. The chapter concludes with a practical guide so that as new research continues to emerge, you become more informed about how to interpret findings and translate them into meaning for your own professional context.

In Chapter 3, we explore what is meant by effective pedagogy. This chapter emphasises the importance of precision in pedagogical vocabulary and highlights the importance of pedagogical alignment – between Pedagogical Beliefs, Intentions, and Practice.

In Chapter 4, we take you on a journey – introducing four personas as a way of introducing Traditional, Individual Constructivist, Social Constructivist, and

Sociocultural Pedagogical Belief systems or stances. We then take you through a guided activity which facilitates a self-discovery process – identifying your own personal Pedagogical Beliefs.

In Chapter 5, we introduce and explain the Funnel of Influences model as a way of recognising and unpacking the many different influences affecting an individual teacher's practice. We then take you through a self-discovery process – identifying influences – both personal and contextual – which affect your use of digital technology to support learning.

In Chapter 6, we introduce key terminology to support thinking more precisely about Pedagogical Practice. We will take you through guided activities which help you to unpack Intended and Enacted Practice when using digital technology – leading to new insights which will enhance your pedagogical effectiveness.

In Chapter 7, we explore how digital technology can be used in significantly different ways depending on the teacher's Pedagogical Beliefs. We guide you through worked examples and illustrations before engaging in a guided activity which unpacks your own practice.

In Chapter 8, we introduce the idea of Pedagogical Alignment Gaps – the misalignment between pedagogical beliefs, intentions and practice. Suggestions are provided about how to increase individual pedagogical alignment, and guided activities are provided to support professional teams to enhance organisational pedagogical alignment.

Chapter 9 highlights the importance of Precision Planning and the ways in which it is possible to bring greater consistency to the Pedagogical Practices that learners experience. It encourages you to form an action plan so that the impact of the book continues into the future.

This book will take you on a supportive journey – first encouraging you to delve deeper into what you believe and what you do in practice and then helping you bring greater alignment between your beliefs, your intentions and your actions.

The provocations in this book are intended to move you beyond your comfort zone as you reflect on your previous practices and see how you have much more control over your future Pedagogical Practices than you might have historically realised …

References

Aubrey-Smith, F. (2021) *An exploration of the relationship between teachers' pedagogical stance and their uses of ICT in classroom practice.* Doctoral Thesis. The Open University.

Buchanan, R. (2020) 'Through Growth to Achievement: Examining EdTech as a Solution to Australia's Declining Educational Achievement', *Policy Futures in Education*, 18(8), pp. 1026–1043.

Butler, D. et al. (2018) 'Education Systems in the Digital Age: The Need for Alignment', *Technology, Knowledge and Learning*, 23(3), pp. 473–494.

Cloke, C. (2000) 'Planning to Use ICT, Factors Which Influence Teachers', *ESRC ICT & Pedagogy*, [Preprint].

Cooper Gibson (2021) *Education Technology (EdTech) Survey 2021*. DfE: London.

Education Endowment Foundation (2019) *Digital Technology to Improve Learning: An Evidence Review*. London: Education Endowment Foundation.

Holon Education Intelligence Unit (2022) *Sizing the Global EdTech Market*. New York: Holon Education Intelligence Unit. https://www.holoniq.com/notes/sizing-the-global-EdTech-market

Kasinathan, G. (2021) 'National Educational Policy 2020 – Imagining Digital Technology as a Resource to Achieve Educational Aims', *Voices of Teachers and Teacher Educators*, X(II), December 2021, pp. 20–28.

Kemp, P., and Berry, M. (2019) *The Roehampton Annual Computing Education Report Pre-Release Snapshot From 2018*. Roehampton: British Computing Society.

Luckin, R. (2018) *Enhancing Learning and Teaching with Technology: What the Research Says*. London: UCL Institute of Education Press.

Maddux, C. D., and Waggoner, M. D. (1993) 'Past and Future Stages in Educational Computing Research', in H. C. Waxman and G. W. Bright (eds) *Approaches to Research on Teacher Education and Technology*. Virginia: Association for the Advancement of Computing in Education, pp. 11–22.

Rhodes, V. (1989) *Barriers to Innovation – A Seminar Report*. Lancaster: ESRC.

Robinson, B. (1993) 'Communicating Through Computers in the Classroom', in P. Scrimshaw (ed.) *Language, Classrooms & Computers*. 1st edn. London: Routledge, pp. 111–129.

Rodriguez, B., Rebeca, M., Romani, C., Cristobal, J., Munoz-Najar, A., Sanchez, C., and Inaki, A. (2022) *Remote Learning During the Global School Lockdown: Multi-Country Lessons (English)*. Washington, D.C.: World Bank Group.

Selwyn, N. (2018) *Telling Tales on Technology: Qualitative Studies of Technology and Education*. 2nd edn. Oxon: Routledge.

Selwyn, N., and Facer, K. (2021) *Digital Technology and the Futures of Education: Towards 'Non-Stupid' Optimism*. Paris: United Nations Background Paper.

Squires, D., and McDougall, A. (1994) *Choosing and Using Educational Software: A Teacher's Guide*. London: Falmer Press.

TALIS (2018) *Teaching and Learning International Survey: insights and Interpretations*. Paris: OECD.

The Royal Society (2017) *After the Reboot: Computing Education in UK Schools*. London: The Royal Society.

Twining, P. (2002) *Enhancing the Impact of Investments in 'Educational' ICT*. PhD Thesis. The Open University.

Twining, P. (2019) *If school is the problem, what is the solution?* Milton Keynes: Open University.

UK Council for Internet Safety (2020) *Education for a Connected World*. London: UKCIS.

Vincentini, L. et al. (2022) *Future Opportunities for Education Technology in England*. London: Department for Education.

CHAPTER

2

What is the evidence telling us?

Introduction

As a busy professional, you have probably turned to this chapter to read a summary of what the latest EdTech research findings are and what you need to do as a result. We have synthesised our top six 'need to know' findings in relation to pedagogy and digital technology, but alongside that, it is important that you are able to make sense of both current and future research.

Therefore, this chapter has three parts:

Part 1 summarises six recommendations that consistently emerge from evidence from research and practice.

Part 2 unpacks some of the embedded (but often ignored) issues within EdTech research.

Part 3 goes 'behind the scenes' of EdTech research and explains why and how research design makes such a big difference to research findings.

The six things you need to know

When we wrote this book, we considered how best to share a synthesis of the many millions of words that have been spoken and written about EdTech. There is an abundance of research that has been published by academics, teachers and school leaders, policy shapers and suppliers. Yet each of these sources often criticises others working in the same space. Academics criticise practitioner materials for a lack of robustness. Practitioners criticise academics for being out of touch with classroom reality. Policy research is criticised for being surface-level or politically biased. Classroom research is criticised for being small-scale and anecdotal.

DOI: 10.4324/9781003321637-2

This makes it very difficult for those of us working in the ecosystem of school digital technology to join together with a coherent future direction.

Our approach, therefore, is to deliberately draw on a very wide range of sources – and we invite you to be similarly open to the breadth and range of insights offered by colleagues across the sector who share your interest in using digital technology effectively to enhance learning.

Here are our top six 'need to know' findings.

1

Who's driving the EdTech bus?
Senior and system leaders should be the ones championing digital technology, not just EdTech enthusiasts. It should be central to school strategic thinking. Furthermore, any decision about digital technology in school should be seen as a pedagogical decision – and should be led by those who understand the pedagogical implications.

2

Know thy Pedagogy
Be absolutely clear about Pedagogical Intentions for supporting learning before considering which digital technology to use (if any) and how to use it. This means each teacher and leader needs to understand their individual Pedagogical Beliefs and how these translate into Pedagogical Practices.

3

An on-demand mindset
For digital technology to be most effective, learners need to have access to devices 'on demand' – as and when learning can be enhanced by their use. This approach is usually strongly influenced by mindsets about classroom power dynamics (which reflect our Pedagogical Beliefs).

4

Trust changes everything
Digital technology changes power relationships in the classroom, giving more power to learners. This better prepares learners to be proactive and take responsibility for their own learning. However, this can be intimidating for learners, teachers, leaders, and parents and may be resisted by some. This is particularly problematic within organisations where there is a lack of trust of learners (and/or teachers). Digital technology offers the most benefit in a context in which learners can be agentive about their own learning.

5

Monitor what you value
Digital technology is often best at supporting learning that is not explicitly captured by existing performance measures (e.g. autonomy, responsibility). In order to know whether the uses of digital technology are adding the greatest value, you first need to be clear about what you value. Then monitor that. For example, whether your priority is preparing young people to be effective citizens in our rapidly changing world or maximising high-stakes test results (although the two are not incompatible!).

The evidence iceberg
Evidence and understanding about learners' needs, and about effective pedagogical approaches to meeting them should be at the heart of all thinking, decision-making, and action. Decisions about digital technology and learning should also be informed by robust evidence from both quantitative and qualitative research. Understanding the complexity of education research and how published findings relate to your own nuanced context really matters. In-depth small-scale studies and practitioner research (that reflect your context) can be more informative than large-scale statistical studies.

The purpose of this book is to champion a pedagogically led approach to using digital technology in schools. These six findings – drawn from theoretical and empirical evidence – set out how this can be achieved. However, to unpack and explore each of these findings meaningfully will require more than one book. Thus, *this* book will take you on a journey that enables you to deeply understand your own Pedagogical Beliefs and the consequent implications for your Pedagogical Practice.

Making sense of EdTech research

There has been a lot of research examining EdTech over a long period. However, there seems to be an assumption that because digital technology itself changes rapidly, related research findings also change very quickly. As Selwyn et al. (2019) point out, this means that sometimes EdTech research doesn't take account of the still-relevant lessons learned from its own history.

Despite the many changes in approaches to exploring EdTech, research findings within the field have not changed substantially over the last few decades (Hammond, 2020; Costa et al., 2019). This reflects the overarching finding that the key issues are not technological ones but issues to do with human factors (Fawns, 2022; Aubrey-Smith, 2021). These change much less rapidly than digital technology.

There are a number of issues embedded within EdTech research which are affecting the way that it has tended to be designed and conducted. Furthermore, as we explain later in this chapter, these issues also directly affect findings and conclusions. These issues include the following:

- The 'What works' agenda, and the importance of context
- A history of focusing on 'what' and 'how' rather than 'why'
- The importance of recognising embedded belief systems
- The difficulties of self-reported data and perceptions of barriers
- The central role of teacher beliefs

The 'what works' agenda and the importance of context

As part of the move towards a more 'evidence informed profession', there has been a shift in education towards utilising a 'what works' approach in research. There are a number of online sources which rank strategies based on the probability that they will be impactful on teaching and learning. For example, the Education Endowment Foundation Teaching and Learning Toolkit (EEF, 2021a) and Visible Learning Meta-analyses (2021).

These create easy-to-access lists of strategies that teachers are encouraged to use to guide their everyday practice. These research findings are useful. However, as those who create them point out (e.g. EEF, 2021b, Hattie, 2023), they should not be used in isolation from other forms of research. This is because

- the 'what works' approach assumes that there is a simple relationship between a specific practice and student performance. This ignores the importance of the many other influences affecting the student, their teacher and the way in which that practice is introduced and implemented within the school.
- translating findings from randomised controlled trials into your own classroom practice is not straightforward – context matters – just think how different any two of your classes have been and what a difference that makes to you and your learners' experiences.
- the 'impact' measures often focus on common performance measures (e.g. test scores or other forms of core subject assessment) which provide a very limited view about the impact on learning, often ignoring aspects that effective digital technology use has the most impact on.
- the 'what works' approach ignores the often unintended side effects (Zhao, 2018), of particular interventions (e.g. teaching synthetic phonics may enhance learner ability to decode text but at the same time reduce their enjoyment of reading).

We only have to look at the classroom of learners in front of us to recognise that this kind of 'what works' approach has its limitations. We know that no learning strategy works for all learners all of the time. In fact, sometimes learners learn 'despite' a particular approach being used! As teachers, we know that learning experiences are complex and multi-faceted. Learners bring with them preconceived ideas about their learning and about themselves as learners, and each of us responds differently to different learners. Different factors affect learners in different ways – the weather, the time of day, the temperature, the previous lesson, the person sitting next to them, how hungry they are. So high-quality research needs to take this into account rather than simply ignore it on the basis of statistics. Human beings are more than just numbers.

As Professor Neil Selwyn (2018) argues, the 'what works' approach draws our attention to what 'could' happen rather than what 'does' happen. The irony of this is that we are then making decisions about the trajectories of learners' lives based on a percentage chance of it being a success. Whilst the 'what works' approach argues that an intervention works for 85% of learners and therefore is worthy of implementing, this is based on the assumption that what worked in the research settings will also work equally well in your class which, as noted earlier, may well not be true.

The key message is that context matters. What works in one place, at one moment in time, with one set of learners may well not work in other places or at other times or with other learners. Furthermore, any improvement to learning is unlikely to be just about one isolated strategy or one new approach. To help unpack this, we have dedicated the whole of Chapter 5 to revealing the many influences that affect digital technology practices – including global, national, school, and classroom contexts and how these interact with individuals' identities.

A history of focusing on 'what' and 'how' rather than 'why'

Literature concerned with the use of digital technology in teaching practices is generally located in one of two areas; summarised as 'the what' and 'the how' (Aubrey-Smith, 2021). The first of these bodies of literature has largely been commissioned by, or linked to policy, funding, or accountability. These studies report on the 'what' – the types of digital technology in schools that appear to be beneficial – thus informing future policy and budget decisions (e.g. OECD, 2021; Haleem et al., 2022; BESA, 2021; Cooper Gibson, 2022b; McKinsey, 2020, EC, 2019). The second body of literature has started to unpick the relationship between digital technology and pedagogy – going beyond the 'what' to probe the 'how'. These publications seek to explain or support the role of digital technology within learning (e.g. Twining et al., 2017a; Mitra, 2014; Luckin, 2012). There is a subset of this body of literature that offers advice on which digital technologies are likely to be most impactful (e.g. EEF, 2020; Nesta, 2019; Stringer et al., 2019). However, by presenting findings in this way, there is an inference that the relative benefits of the software (the what) are what will make an impact on learning rather than the actions of the teacher or learners using it (the how). Thus, the focus remains very much on the technology (the what) despite often being prefaced with a literature review that recognises that the 'how' should be the focus. None of these focus deeply on the 'why'.

The importance of recognising embedded belief systems

Another notable trend across EdTech research is that teachers are consistently provoked to do *something* in relation to digital technology, arguably a natural consequence of policy, investment, and/or cultural expectation (Fernandez-Batanero et al., 2021; Spiteri et al., 2020; Luckin, 2018). Whilst school staff almost unanimously agree that integrating digital technology into learning and teaching is necessary (OUP, 2021), digital technology has not yet become embedded, and its use within and across schools remains variable (CooperGibson, 2022a; EC, 2019). Given that global studies (e.g. OUP, 2022) have shown that teacher confidence in their digital skills has doubled since pre-pandemic (from 43% to 93%), it is vitally important that colleagues are meaningfully supported so that confidence translates into meaningful learning experiences for our young people.

As Hammond (2014) argued, the largely consistent rationale behind initiatives to promote digital technology is an assumption that it can have a positive impact on standards, that it can provide more vocational relevance in the curriculum, or that it can be a catalyst for curriculum reform. One of the central challenges to these ideas, he argues, is that enthusiasts think that it is digital technology itself which is making a difference, rather than recognising that actions are prompted by the values and beliefs of human beings. We – both individually and collectively – become catalysts or barriers to change through the choices that we make about how to implement digital technology use.

In parallel to this, there is an ongoing debate about whether living out specific kinds of practice in a sustained and focused way might eventually (but doesn't necessarily) reshape our values or beliefs (e.g. Halstead and Taylor, 2000). For example, Buchanan (2020) highlights the ways in which using digital technology can (but doesn't necessarily) prompt changes to wider behaviours through repeated actions and embedded value systems.

These findings about embedded value systems create an important backdrop to how we then view research concerned with EdTech. Yet the significant majority of publications do not yet recognise this influence (Beckman et al., 2019; Selwyn, 2018). Perhaps this is because historically those who commission, fund and conduct EdTech research have often done so from a technology, policy, or commercial backdrop – domains usually focused on processes or products rather than explicit philosophies (e.g. CooperGibson, 2022a).

One of the ways that this issue impacts EdTech research is that it encourages the externalisation of catalysts and barriers to the effective use of digital technology.

The difficulties of self-reported data and perceptions of barriers

There is a historical trend within EdTech research to depend on self-reported quantitative studies (often large-scale online surveys completed by teachers and leaders). However, Abernethy (2015) invites us to think carefully about findings that researchers draw from this kind of data generation by considering it from a psychological perspective. Each of us responds differently based on what kinds of questions are presented and how they are phrased and, importantly (yet often subconsciously), who we think will act as a result of the survey outcomes. We may be prompted to remember or prioritise certain things as a result of particular questions in the survey. Furthermore, the survey may intentionally *not* prompt us to offer insights into things which could be very relevant.

Let's think about a practical example. If we are being surveyed about barriers to the use of digital technology by a policy or funding body, we may respond in a way that we think will affect change (i.e. by citing the need for more resources and training). As Hoskin (2012) points out, surveys asking teachers about barriers to digital technology use which give equipment and internet access as response options are unlikely to provoke introspection about educational or personal related barriers (i.e. teaching and learning decisions). That kind of survey is framing the teacher to see the barriers as external to themselves rather than relating to their own beliefs or actions – and is therefore 'leading the findings' in a particular direction according to the researcher's own agenda or objectives.

These kinds of studies encourage and perpetuate a trend within EdTech research to externalise catalysts and barriers to effective digital technology use. For example, highlighting issues to do with access to connectivity (e.g. Warioba et al., 2021; Jerrim and Sims, 2019), the role of leadership and management (e.g. Peled & Perzon, 2021; Talip & Tiop, 2020), time and capacity (e.g. Lucas et al., 2021), concerns about student behaviour (e.g. Nikolopoulou et al., 2022), and digital skills training (e.g. Belay, 2020; Ifinedo et al., 2020; Sánchez-Prieto et al., 2019).

Research which encourages us to see barriers to the use of digital technology as unrelated to local and personal influences are problematic. For example, a commonly cited barrier to using digital technology relates to connectivity and device access. However, when these data were probed across 13 countries, Light and Pierson (2012) found that once a minimal standard of infrastructure was in place, then the presence of digital technology itself made an insignificant difference to the frequency and the nature of use within teaching. This is a highly relevant finding because the minimal standard of infrastructure was below what the majority of UK schools have access to (BESA, 2020). This finding is supported in the most recent large-scale TALIS data (e.g. TALIS, 2018) which found that even in schools with a comprehensive Information Technology (IT) infrastructure, there were often very low levels of digital technology use.

Let's take a localised example. Data from the DfE (2022) and BESA (2022) suggest that there are approximately 6 million laptops, computers, and tablets in schools in England and about 9 million pupils. However, even in schools which have 1:1 device provision, usage data tends to vary. Therefore, whilst devices and usage rates are not evenly distributed, these findings suggest that even if there was a device for every student in every school, there would still be more questions to ask. It is important to remember that with any digital technology, just because we have access to it doesn't mean it is being used meaningfully.

In Chapter 5, we introduce you to the Funnels of Influence which will help you unpack what is influencing digital technology use in your own context.

The central role of teacher beliefs

Most contemporary research recognises that the greatest influence to the meaningful use of digital technology in the classroom is the teacher themself (e.g. EEF, 2020).

However, as Tang (2021) reports, there is often still a trend in the research to externalise the issues relating to this influence – focusing on training and capacity rather than teachers' beliefs and intentions. This is where looking holistically at the research field matters. When thinking about the dynamics between teachers and digital technology, therefore, we need to remember that teachers will have embedded values and beliefs that inform their uses of digital technology and that these may or may not lead to practice that is conceived by themselves or others as 'effective'. In other words, teachers' values and beliefs are central to their use of digital technology.

Tondeur et al. (2017) undertook a systematic review of qualitative evidence exploring the relationship between teachers' Pedagogical Beliefs and digital technology use in education. There were five synthesised findings:

- the relationship between Pedagogical Beliefs and digital technology use should be seen as bidirectional, with digital technology use creating, reconstructing, or reaffirming beliefs
- teachers' Pedagogical Beliefs may hinder or prevent digital technology integration – for example, teachers with Traditional beliefs are less likely to adopt digital technology
- teachers are more likely to adopt digital technology that best suits their needs at a particular moment in time
- there is very little in the way of understanding of the role of Pedagogical Beliefs when considering professional development and digital technology
- not all teachers within the same school hold the same Pedagogical Beliefs, and whilst both a teacher and their school may have positive or negative views towards digital technology, it does not necessarily mean that one causes the other.

In Chapter 4, we guide you through what different Pedagogical Beliefs look like, how to unpack and explore your own Pedagogical Beliefs, and what the implications are for future practice.

In the previous section, we guided you through some of the embedded issues within the vast range of published EdTech research. However, this is an ever-expanding space, and it is important that you approach future research findings with a critical lens. The next part of this chapter explains some key points to bear in mind when trying to make sense of the published research literature.

A short guide to interpreting EdTech research

One of the great developments in education over more recent years has been the way in which access to published research has been made increasingly available to school-based educators. Bodies such as the EEF, Visible Learning, the National Foundation for Educational Research, and universities worldwide have published summaries and made searchable databases publicly available, and there are a growing number of open-access journals accessible (e.g. via the University of Melbourne, 2022 and JSTOR, 2022). This allows us all to consume readily available research findings to inform our classroom practice (for more, see Twining & Aubrey-Smith, 2021).

In parallel to this, our teaching profession has become increasingly enthusiastic about practitioner research – with the emergence of research-invested schools[1] and practitioner research hubs and networks growing alongside engagement in postgraduate research courses (Universities UK, 2022; HESA, 2021; HEPI, 2020). This presents huge opportunities for teachers and school leaders to both consume and create research (Twining et al., 2022). But it also demands that already busy professionals learn and develop yet another set of skills in order to avoid biased approaches, misconceptions, and applications of ideas in ways which might be counterproductive to learning.

Here are some key things that you need to know about how to interpret research.

Theoretical stance and methodology

One of the key messages across the research is that the nature of research fundamentally impacts its findings (Avenier and Thomas, 2015). Therefore, in this part of this chapter, we walk you through the following:

- The Quantitative versus Qualitative debate – and why it matters in EdTech research
- Research designs – who chooses the methods and why they choose them
- Different types of research outcomes and what they might mean for you

Finally, we provide you with a set of questions to help you critically read any EdTech research. Our aim is to equip you with the information you need in order to be able to make sense of the literature and make evidence-based decisions about your future actions.

Table 2.1 provides an overview of key research terminology that we use and how different elements within the research process relate to each other. A lack of precision in how terminology is used has been a major problem in educational research (Twining, 2010). Defining terms in this way allows greater precision and a shared understanding when describing and understanding different theoretical stances and different approaches to research.

The quantitative versus qualitative debate

All of us have underlying beliefs about the nature of reality (our ontology) and beliefs about how we come to know the world (our epistemology). Researchers are no different to anyone else in this respect. So it's important to understand that these beliefs directly shape the way that people carry out research and the way that we then interpret their findings. Our beliefs inform our choices.

Table 2.1 Research terminology (Twining, 2018)

	Level		Contrasting stances	
Theoretical stance	**Ontology** Beliefs about the nature of being or reality		There is one objective reality	There are multiple realities
Theoretical stance	**Epistemology** Belief about the nature and scope of knowledge (How we come to know the world)		You uncover the reality – there is one true explanation	Meaning is culturally defined
Approach	**Methodology**		**Quantitative** Positivist, Objectivist, Empiricist, Nomothetic	**Qualitative** Hermeneutic Interpretivist
Approach	**Design**		Experimental Quasi-experimental Random Controlled Trials	Case study Action research Ethnography
Approach	**Emphasises**		Deductive reasoning	Inductive reasoning
Approach	**Data** (numerical or non-numerical)	**Methods**	Techniques for collecting data, such as survey/questionnaire, interview/focus group, document analysis, observation	
Approach		**Instruments**	Specific data collection tools, such as a specific questionnaire or interview schedule	
Approach		**Analysis**	How the data are processed in order to make sense of them (to answer your research questions)	
Approach	**Outcomes**		Generalisable Statistics can't answer the 'why' question	Relevant/Resonate Build theory (answer the 'why' question)

Some examples of the different belief systems that underpin educational research include the following:

- Positivist paradigm – believing that there are hidden rules or truths that can be uncovered by using reliable and valid ('scientific') methods
- Interpretivist paradigm – believing that reality is socially constructed and that there are multiple realities, with meaning being reconstructed through interpretation of the interactions between the researcher and the research subjects

- Critical realist paradigm – believing that inequality and injustice permeate society and should be exposed using approaches best suited to the needs of the research.

Each of these belief systems defines how a researcher then conceptualises their research. That conceptualisation is known as a research methodology.

> For a more detailed exploration of research paradigms in educational contexts, see Kivunja, C., & Kuyini, A.B. (2017) Understanding and Applying Research Paradigms in Educational Contexts. *International Journal of Higher Education*, *6*(5), pp.26–41.

A research methodology frames 'how' we are carrying out a particular study, the methods that we use to generate data, how we analyse that data, and the sorts of outcomes or claims that we make based on our findings (Twining et al., 2017b). You are probably aware of two common methodologies – quantitative and qualitative.

Quantitative research is underpinned by positivist beliefs that there is one objective reality and that the job of research is to uncover the one true explanation of that reality. Thus, quantitative researchers seek the single explanation for a phenomenon – the role of research is uncovering it – as if there is a hidden treasure already out there waiting to be found. Quantitative research can use non-numerical data but usually uses numerical data. However, numerical data and quantitative research are not interchangeable terms (numerical data can be used in other methodologies too). The key thing to remember about quantitative research is that its epistemology (the nature of reality) and ontology (how we come to know the world) are always positivist. Quantitative research will almost always focus on issues such as validity, reliability, transferability, and generalisability (which are explained later).

Qualitative research is underpinned by a relativist or an interpretivist stance – the belief that there are multiple realities and that the role of research is to help us understand these different perspectives. Qualitative research recognises that context is central and critical – and that meaning is culturally defined. This sort of interpretivist approach asks *why* something is happening and seeks to surface and unpack the influences affecting a given situation in order to understand it more meaningfully. Whilst qualitative research usually uses non-numerical data (e.g. what people say or are observed doing), it can also use numerical data. Irrespective of the data used, the underpinning theoretical stance is a relativist one – analysis recognises the importance of context when interpreting meanings in the data set. Whilst some qualitative research refers to validity and reliability, more helpful terms are transparency, trustworthiness, and credibility (which are explained later). Qualitative researchers do not claim that their findings will generalise or transfer unproblematically to other contexts; rather, they aim to provide insights that may be relevant in similar contexts and/or to develop theory (i.e. explanations of why things work in the way that they do).

These two methodological stances – quantitative and qualitative – are often set in opposition to each other because of their different underlying assumptions about the nature of reality and how you can investigate it. However, this is unhelpful because it sometimes means that we ignore great swathes of research evidence. Indeed, the need to redress the imbalance between quantitative and qualitative EdTech research has been highlighted by experts (Pérez-Sanagustin et al., 2017), and the ideal solution is for us to use a combination of both.

Different methodologies (i.e. quantitative or qualitative) lend themselves to different research designs. In the next section, a number of key designs are explained in terms of the purposes that they are usually used for, the methods that are generally employed, and how data are typically analysed. The strengths and limitations of the different designs are then outlined, and the sorts of outcomes they produce are described.

Designs

Views of what counts as credible research have changed over the years. There has been a marked shift since the turn of the century towards quantitative designs such as trials (particularly randomised controlled trials [RCTs]) and mixed methods, and away from taking into account qualitative research designs such as case studies and practitioner research. As we explore these different designs below you will see that they each have advantages and limitations. Shifts in which designs are fashionable do not necessarily reflect their ability to help us understand what is happening and why.

> For a more comprehensive explanation of the differences between different types of research and their associated terminology. see Twining, P. et al. (2017b) 'Some Guidance on Conducting and Reporting Qualitative Studies', Computers & Education, 106, pp. A1–A9.

Trials (including RCTs)

Trials are quasi-experimental studies which at their simplest involve testing the impacts of an intervention on a group of learners. Well-designed trials will also have a control group who do not experience the intervention but undergo a comparable experience to the intervention that is being tested. Trials generally involve the use of a pre-test to establish what the learners know (or can do) before the intervention (or comparable experience) and a post-test to see how their knowledge (or what they can do) has changed after the intervention. The purpose of a trial is to establish the efficacy of the intervention. Conclusions are drawn by analysing data using statistics to see whether there is a correlation between the intervention and significant differences in 'learning gains' (as measured by the pre- and post-test results) between the experimental and control groups.

RCTs are trials that aim to randomly allocate participants to different groups with the aim of eliminating some sources of bias. RCTs have one or more control groups who are compared with participants in one of more experimental groups who undergo the intervention(s). RCTs generally involve large numbers of participants. They are based on the medical model of testing new drugs by comparing their effects on patients who take the drugs with those who take a placebo. Ideally, in trials, the members of the control and experimental groups are not aware of which group they are in and thus whether they are experiencing the intervention that is being tested or not.

The assumption is that if a trial/RCT has been carried out rigorously then the findings can be generalised – they can be applied to other learners in other contexts. Rigour is often couched in terms of the validity and reliability of the study. Validity has several elements, which relate to the extent to which the study actually measures what it is claiming to measure, and whether the participants in the study are deemed to be representative of the wider population and thus the findings will apply to the wider population (they can be generalised). Reliability relates to the extent to which the study could be replicated (repeated and come to the same conclusions).

Quantitative studies such as RCTs give us surface-level 'big picture' findings – that make something 'more likely' to happen 'if' a specific set of criteria are in place. We have to be careful when using these findings. If an RCT reported that 98% of learners improved in their times tables tests when using an online times tables game, then we might be tempted to start using that game in order to see those kinds of learning gains in our own learners. However, if the RCT was comparing learners using the times tables game with learners not doing any times tables practice, then it's not the game itself that had the impact – it's that the learners were practising their times tables. Furthermore, if the learners that took part in the RCT were taking part because their school was prioritising times tables as part of a whole school improvement strategy, then we would expect to see some gains with all the attention being placed on times tables.

RCTs also assume that

- both the control group and trial group are equivalent (if given the same intervention then they would both have the same change in test results between the pre- and post-tests);
- the interventions experienced by both groups are equivalent;
- there are no other variables that might have an impact on the post-test performance (e.g. learners in one group might do some additional study outside class which impacts their post-test results);
- the learners in the experimental condition are no more highly motivated than the control group even if they are doing something new; and
- there is no Hawthorne effect – where outcomes are impacted simply by an awareness that performance is being observed.

Mixed methods

Another quantitative methodology commonly used is 'mixed methods'. As the name suggests, this uses a range of methods to generate a mix of numerical and non-numerical data (e.g. a trial or a questionnaire, plus interviews). Most mixed methods studies are underpinned by a positivist stance where there is a 'truth' out there that can be discovered and then transferred to other contexts. Within mixed-methods studies, non-numerical data are often converted into numerical data and analysed statistically (e.g. counting the number of respondents who answered survey or interview questions in ways that could be considered 'the same' as each other). As with other quantitative research, mixed-methods studies are concerned with validity and reliability and suggest that results can be generalised to the wider population.

Case studies

Case studies are a research design that enables the researcher to explore a phenomenon in situ. They generally use a range of methods, including one or more questionnaires, interviews, observations, and document analysis (e.g. policy documents, lesson plans, samples of learners' work). The purpose of case studies is to develop a rich description of what is happening that enables the researcher to infer causal relationships. The data generated are usually non-numerical (e.g. audio recordings of interviews, video recordings of observations, samples of work) but may include some numerical data (e.g. estimates of how long digital technology was in use). Analysis of the data generally involves looking for repeating patterns – often by coding the data to group ideas (e.g. data about x) and then cross-checking to see if any of the data do not fit with the identified themes.

Unlike quantitative studies, which tend to ignore contextual influences, case studies recognise that context profoundly affects the generation and interpretation of data. This means that you cannot replicate a case study as the contextual detail will always be different. This is true even if you are working with the same participants – they will not be 'the same' next time because their experiences will have changed their ideas. If you have taught 'the same lesson' to two different groups of learners you will know that the lesson isn't 'the same' – it becomes taught slightly differently, and the learners respond slightly differently. Even if those differences are subtle, they mean that the two versions are not 'the same'. Thus, the notion of reliability is problematic for qualitative research. This doesn't mean that qualitative research isn't rigorous but instead that rigour is demonstrated by being transparent – being very clear – about how the research was conducted and what the influences were within it.

Qualitative research also challenges the notion of a study being 'valid'. This is partly because the individuality and unique nature of participants is acknowledged. This means that the idea of participants 'being representative' in the sense of being 'the same' as other non-participants is illogical. Furthermore, qualitative research recognises that there may be more than one possible interpretation of what is happening. This means that rather than conclusions offering a 'right answer', the researcher instead demonstrates to their reader that their findings are credible and trustworthy. A qualitative researcher would not propose that findings are generalisable (in the sense of automatically applying to other contexts or people). Instead, the researcher would offer insights and findings of potential relevance to readers.

Practitioner research (including action research)

Practitioner research, of which action research is one particular design, aims to investigate and improve classroom practice. This often involves the practitioner changing some aspect of their teaching in order to address an issue that they are interested in. Practitioner research is an extension of reflective practice, which additionally (a) draws on what is already known about an issue by the professional knowledge base and (b) contributes information back to that professional knowledge base. These connections with the wider profession are vitally important in terms of sharing expertise, and help to position teachers as experts and teaching as a profession.

Who chooses which designs, and why do they choose them?

Different research designs are used for different purposes and require varying levels of resourcing to carry them out. As all research requires researcher time, there will always be a person or organisation facilitating that researcher capacity. This could be

- research for professional development,
- research undertaken as part of postgraduate study (e.g. EdD or PhD),
- university research that is not externally funded,
- research funded by a research council,
- research funded by an EdTech supplier,
- research commissioned by a politically oriented body, or
- research commissioned for media or commercial purposes.

The person or organisation facilitating the research usually defines the budget available, the person or body leading the research, and the nature of the objectives and desirable outcomes (e.g. a preference towards quantitative or qualitative methodologies). These embed forms of bias from the outset which can affect research methodology, design, data generated, analysis, and the nature of conclusions. For example,

- Trials are relatively cheap and quick to carry out. They are often used by bodies who want to test a particular intervention on a small scale.
- RCTs are large-scale studies which are more expensive and can be time-consuming. They are generally carried out by a team of researchers and/or consultants who are funded by government agencies or other politically or media-oriented organisations.
- Mixed-methods studies often use questionnaires which are relatively quick and easy and therefore relatively cheap to deploy and analyse, alongside a small number of interviews relating to a subset of the questionnaire respondents. Interviews are quite time-consuming to carry out but superficial analysis (such as counting how many times respondents said x) is relatively quick and easy.
- Case studies tend to be time-consuming because they rely heavily on interviewing and observation which takes a lot of researcher time. They may be

carried out by individual researchers or where multiple case study sites are involved by a team of researchers and consultants. In-depth analysis of interviews and observations is very time-consuming.

- Practitioner research is generally carried out by an individual teacher or small team within a school who want to enhance some aspect of their practice or overcome a specific issue. Carrying out practitioner research adds a layer of complexity to the already-challenging task of teaching, but it is one of the most effective forms of professional learning (Twining, 2019) and helps position teachers as experts in education because they are contributing to the professional knowledge base. Sharing the findings from practitioner research is an important part of the process – if you don't share it, then it isn't research.

When a study is funded by an organisation that has a vested interest in the outcomes, there will be embedded influence and potential bias. For example, it is clearly advantageous for a commercial organisation if research shows their product to be effective.

Suppliers of high-quality digital technology are increasingly providing insights into the design and purpose of their products. However, it is important to be discerning about their findings. Many suppliers use vague phrases such as 'supports pedagogy', but it is not realistic to evaluate a product in isolation from the Pedagogical Beliefs of the person gatekeeping its use in practice (i.e. teacher, leader, developer, product trainer).

As Beckman (2018) argues, it is a mistake to invest digital technology with objective qualities rather than recognising them as being socially constructed. This does not mean that we should not use product-centred research. However, it does mean that we need to interpret such studies by looking at the evidence presented with a critical lens. At the end of this chapter, we provide you with a guide for how to interpret any kind of research and how to draw out findings that are meaningful for your own specific context.

Outcomes

Different research designs tend to result in different kinds of outcomes.

Quantitative studies tend to result in statistically verified outcomes, which may be in terms of

- improvements in performance due to specific interventions ('what works')
- identification of factors that have an impact on a phenomenon (impact factors or barriers) and/or
- frameworks that show relationships between factors.

These kinds of outcomes make quick and easy-to-understand headlines, and so are the preferred outcomes of political, media, and often commercial organisations.

We often see these kinds of research outcomes in news headlines, policy documents, accountability materials, and corporate publications.

Quantitative studies often identify correlations between variables; for example more learners in a classroom might correlate with more noise. However, having a lot of learners in a classroom does not automatically mean that there will be a lot of noise. Correlations do not necessarily indicate causality.

Qualitative studies tend to produce models, insights, and/or causal explanations (theories). These kinds of outcomes take more time to digest and so are often seen as more academic or for discussion purposes. We often see these kinds of research outcomes in roundtable summaries, larger publications (e.g. books), professional workshops, and course materials.

Using the same example of a noisy classroom, the qualitative study might identify the cause of the noise and describe what had influenced one or more learners to create that particular amount of noise.

Causal explanations (theories)

A theory is an explanation of a phenomenon. At its simplest, a theory explains how and why something happens in the way that it does. Quantitative research can highlight correlations between variables, which may warrant further investigation using a qualitative methodology. Qualitative research enables you to probe deeply below the surface of phenomena to understand how and why something is happening in the way that it does – this can generate theory.

Systematic reviews

Whilst not actually an outcome of research, systematic reviews aim to provide a summary of key findings from the literature. In order to do this, they follow a clearly defined process, which sets out how relevant research papers were identified and the criteria that were used to include and exclude particular papers. Usually these criteria eliminate much, if not all, of the qualitative research because the systematic review process often involves combining statistical findings from multiple sources in order to draw conclusions about what works – and thus only include quantitative studies.

Organisations such as the Education Endowment Foundation in England and the What Works Clearinghouse in the US often commission systematic reviews (as well as RCTs) and generally adopt a 'what works' approach to educational research. Their aim, like that of the Australian Education Research Organisation, is to help practitioners by summarising the research literature and providing clear messages about what 'effective practice' looks like. As noted earlier, education is complex, and simplistic interpretations of research findings can be misleading. Eliminating qualitative research removes an important body of evidence about how and why digital technology is being used and the impacts that use is having in particular contexts.

Summary

In this part of the chapter, we have explored some of the different designs and methods used by researchers when conducting research into EdTech. It is our hope that you will use this knowledge to become a discerning consumer of research whether it is produced by academics, suppliers, policy shapers, or practitioner colleagues.

Table 2.2 provides an at-a-glance summary of the details set out earlier which we hope that you will find useful as a reference tool in your future research consumption and creation.

Interpreting research yourself

As you can see, making sense of EdTech research requires you to navigate a complex field, in which you will almost certainly find contradictory evidence.

The best use of evidence is a combination of quantitative and qualitative approaches – which seek to shine a light on the gaps unseen by the other. But if we want to be highly effective users of research, we must challenge all evidence to identify what is most relevant and useful for addressing the needs of the learners in front of us today – our learners.

To help you to do this, we offer you a handy table in the following activity to take you step-by-step through any piece of research – adapted from Twining and Aubrey-Smith (2021).

Guided Activity 2.1: Interpreting research

Choose a piece of research which you are already familiar with. It might be a well-known article or book that your school has used to inform Teaching and Learning strategies or a specific article that you have recently read about an aspect of classroom practice.

Take this opportunity to revisit it with a more critical lens, asking the following questions (Table 2.3).

> We strongly recommend you use the editable version of this Guided Activity, which you can download from www.onelifelearning.co.uk/resources

You are encouraged to use these question prompts as you read and reflect on books, articles, podcasts, news reports, and papers in future. You will find that this helps to develop an increasing sense of what researchers refer to as criticality – balanced, discerning, cautious, and robust interpretation.

> The Monash Q project provides a range of resources to support schools in making more effective use of research evidence.
> (https://www.monash.edu/education/research/projects/qproject/q-suite)

Table 2.2 Summary of key aspects of research

Theoretical stance	**One reality which is to be uncovered**			**Multiple realities, meaning is culturally defined**	
Methodology	**Quantitative**			**Qualitative**	
Design	**Trials**	**Randomised controlled trials**	**Mixed methods**	**Case studies**	**Practitioner research**
Purpose	Testing a product	Trying to bring about systemic change (e.g. save money)	Factors/ barriers/ Perceptions	Trying to understand what is happening and why	Trying to solve a problem/improve practice
Methods	'Control variables' Control/Experimental groups Pre-test, Intervention, Post-test	Random allocation to groups then as Trails.	Survey Interviews	Survey Interview Observation Document analysis	Identify problem Intervention
Analysis	Statistical analysis			Coding/Themes	Reflection
Breadth vs Depth	Neither	Breadth – large scale (helps reduce bias)	Breadth – large number of respondents	Depth (not breadth)	
Credibility	Statistics are seen as credible Credibility is in terms of validity and reliability			Needs to be demonstrated through: ■ transparency about data generation and analysis ■ clearly showing how conclusions were drawn and the richness of the data	

(Continued)

Table 2.2 (Continued)

Theoretical stance	**One reality which is to be uncovered**			**Multiple realities, meaning is culturally defined**	
Design	**Trials**	**Randomised controlled trials**	**Mixed methods**	**Case studies**	**Practitioner research**
Strengths	Statistical analysis is relatively easy		Quick and easy	Can probe causality	Pedagogically focused Best form of professional learning Positions teachers as experts
	Clear-cut results (statistical significance)			Recognises context	
Limitations	Assumptions about samples being representative	Expensive	Ambiguity of questions Self-reporting Superficial (no depth)	Time-consuming	Not seen as an essential part of teaching as a profession – Sharing findings often seen as an add on
	Ignores context You can't control variables – lack of nuance Doesn't consider negative side effects		Often value laden	Need to demonstrate trustworthiness and credibility	
	Can show relationships but correlation is not the same as causality				
Biases (Who does it, who funds it/what is the agenda, why?)	EdTech providers Consultants Academics/PhDs	Government agencies Academics/Consultants (funded by government agencies)	EdTech providers Government agencies Consultants Academics/PhDs	Academics/PhDs	Teachers
Outcomes/ Dissemination	'What works'		'Barriers' Frameworks	Insights/Models/ Theory	Insights

Table 2.3 Questions to ask about published research

Focus	Questions to ask	Your notes
The research question	What is the study trying to find out?	
Potential biases	Who funded the research? Who carried out the research? Why did they do the research? What biases might they have had? How might those have affected the research?	
What is already known about the issue?	Have they explored findings from previous research? Do they consider and weigh up contrasting studies? Have they excluded studies that don't include statistical data? (Many systematic reviews exclude qualitative research.)	
Philosophical stance	What is the underpinning theoretical stance? (Positivist – Interpretivist)	
Design	Is the research design appropriate? Have they clearly explained what they did? (Could you copy the procedure?) Were they rigorous? Were they ethical?	

(Continued)

Table 2.3 (Continued)

Focus	Questions to ask	Your notes
Analysis	Do they clearly explain how they analysed the data in a way that is transparent and credible? Do you have a feel for the scope and depth of the data? Have they probed below the surface to explore different interpretations? Have they demonstrated consideration of all of their data or cherry-picked bits that fit the story they are telling?	
Findings	Are the conclusions based on the data that they actually collected? (You would be surprised how often research conclusions go beyond what the data analysis shows!) Would you have come to the same opinions based on the data they presented?	
Discussion	Do they discuss how their findings relate to findings in the existing literature? Do their findings align with or contradict what is already known, and if they contradict previous research, do they explain and justify why their conclusions are more credible?	
Relevance	Do they clearly describe the context of their research and the kind of participants they were researching? In what ways do they have features in common with your learners and your context? How relevant is the research to your specific context – including your current learners? Are there insights that might be relevant or challenge your thinking even if their context is different to yours?	

Note

1 For example, see http://www.researchinvestedschools.net/

References

Abernethy, M. (2015) 'Self-reports and Observer Reports as Data Generation Methods: An Assessment of Issues of Both Methods', *Universal Journal of Psychology*, 3(1), pp. 22–27.

Aubrey-Smith, F. (2021) *An exploration of the relationship between teachers' pedagogical stance and their use of ICT in classroom practice*. Doctoral thesis. Open University.

Avenier, M., and Thomas, C. (2015) 'Finding One's Way Around Various Methods and Guidelines for Doing Rigorous Qualitative Research: A Comparison of four Epistemological Frameworks', *Systèmes d'Information et Management (French Journal of Management Information Systems)*, 20(1).

Beckman, K., Bennett, S., and Lockyer, L. (2019) 'Reproduction and Transformation of Students' Technology Practice: The Tale of Two Distinctive Secondary Student Cases, *British Journal of Educational Technology*, 50(6), pp. 3315–3328.

Beckman, K. et al. (2018) 'Conceptualising Technology Practice in Education Using Bourdieu's Sociology', *Learning, Media and Technology*, 43(2), pp. 197–210.

Belay, M. T., Khatete, D. W., and Mugo, B. C. (2020) 'Teachers' Skills for ICT Integration in Teaching and Learning', *African Journal of Education and Practice*, 6(2), pp. 44–61.

British Educational Suppliers Association (2020) *Key UK Education Statistics*. London: BESA.

British Educational Suppliers Association (2021) *Insights Archive*. London: BESA.

British Educational Suppliers Association (2022) *Key UK Education Statistics*. London: BESA.

Buchanan, R., (2020) 'Through Growth to Achievement: Examining EdTech as a Solution to Australia's Declining Educational Achievement'. *Policy Futures in Education*, 18(8), pp. 1026–1043.

CooperGibson (2022a) *Education Technology: Exploring Digital Maturity in Schools: Research Report*. London: Department for Education.

CooperGibson (2022b) *The Implementation of Educational Technology in Schools and Colleges*. London: Department for Education.

Costa, C., Hammond, M., and Younie, S. (2019) 'Theorising Technology in Education: An Introduction', *Technology, Pedagogy and Education*, 28(4), pp. 395–399.

Department for Education (2022) *School and Pupil Numbers*. London: Department for Education.

Education Endowment Foundation (2020) *Using Digital Technology to Improve Learning*. London: Education Endowment Foundation.

Education Endowment Foundation (2021a) *Teaching and Learning Toolkit.* https://educationendowmentfoundation.org.uk/education-evidence/teaching-learning-toolkit

Education Endowment Foundation (2021b) *Using the Toolkits.* https://educationendowmentfoundation.org.uk/education-evidence/using-the-toolkits

European Commission (2019) *2nd Survey of Schools: ICT in Education: Shaping Europe's Digital Future.* Brussels: European Commission.

Fawns, T., (2022) 'An Entangled Pedagogy: Looking Beyond the Pedagogy – Technology Dichotomy', *Postdigital Science and Education*, 4(3), pp. 711–728.

Fernández-Batanero, J.-M., Román-Graván, P., Reyes-Rebollo, M.-M., and Montenegro-Rueda, M. (2021) 'Impact of Educational Technology on Teacher Stress and Anxiety: A Literature Review', *International Journal of Environmental Research and Public Health*, 18(2), p. 548.

Haleem, A., Javaid, M., Asim Qadri, M., and Suman, R. (2022) 'Understanding the Role of Digital Technologies in Education: A Review', *Sustainable Operations and Computers*, 3, pp. 275–285.

Halstead, J. M., and Taylor, M. J. (2000) *The Development of Values, Attitudes and Personal Qualities: A Review of Recent Research.* Slough: National Foundation for Educational Research.

Hammond, M. (2014) 'Introducing ICT in Schools in England: Rationale and Consequences', *British Journal of Educational Technology*, 45(2), pp. 191–201.

Hammond, M. (2020) 'What is an Ecological Approach and How Can it Assist in Understanding ICT Take-up?', *British Journal of Educational Technology*, 51(3), pp. 853–866.

Hattie, J. (2023) *Visible Learning: The Sequel A Synthesis of Over 2,100 Meta-Analyses Relating to Achievement.* London: Routledge.

Higher Education Policy Institute (2020) *Landmark report on the last decade of UK postgraduate education provides an indication of what is to come after Covid-19.*

Higher Education Statistics Agency (2021) *Higher Education Student Statistics.* London: HESA.

Hoskin, R. (2012) 'The Dangers of Self-Report', *British Science Association.* http://www.sciencebrainwaves.com/uncategorized/the-dangers-of-self-report

Ifinedo, E., Rikala, J., and Hämäläinen, T. (2020) 'Factors Affecting Nigerian Teacher Educators' Technology Integration: Considering Characteristics, Knowledge Constructs, ICT Practices and Beliefs', *Computers & Education*, 146, Article 103760.

Jerrim, J., and Sims, S. (2019) *The Teaching and Learning International Survey (TALIS) 2018.* Paris: Teaching and Learning International Survey.

JSTOR (2022) *Open and Free Content on JSTOR.* https://about.jstor.org/oa-and-free/

Kivunja, C., and Kuyini, A.B. (2017) 'Understanding and Applying Research Paradigms in Educational Contexts', *International Journal of Higher Education*, 6(5), pp. 26–41.

Light, D., and Pierson, E. (2012) 'The Impact of School Technology Infrastructure on Teacher's Technology Integration: A Survey in Thirteen Countries', *Ubiquitous Learning: An International Journal*, 5(4), pp. 29–40.

Lucas, M., Bem-Haja, P., Siddiq, F., Moreira, A., and Redecker, C., (2021) 'The Relation Between In-Service Teachers' Digital Competence and Personal and Contextual Factors: What Matters Most?', *Computers & Education*, 160(2021), Article 104052.

Luckin, R. (2018) *Enhancing Learning and Teaching with Technology: What the Research Says*. London: UCL Institute of Education Press.

Luckin, R. et al. (2012) *Decoding Learning: The Proof, Promise and Potential of Digital Education*. London: Nesta.

McKinsey (2020) *New Global Data Reveal Education Technology's Impact on Learning*. London: McKinsey.

Mitra, S. (2014) 'The Future of Schooling: Children and Learning at the Edge of Chaos', *Prospects*, 44(4), pp. 547–558.

Nesta (2019) *Making the Most of Technology in Education*. London: Nesta.

Nikolopoulou, K., Gialamas, V., and Lavidas, K. (2022) 'Mobile Learning-technology Barriers in School Education: Teachers' Views', *Technology, Pedagogy and Education*. Published ahead of print. https://doi.org/10.1080/1475939X.2022.2121314

Organisation for Economic Co-operation and Development (2021) *Digital Education Outlook*. Paris: OECD.

Oxford University Press (2021) *Addressing the Deepening Digital Divide*. Oxford: OUP.

Oxford University Press (2022) *Education: The Journey Towards a Digital Revolution: Drawing on Insights and Research from Around the World*. Oxford: OUP.

Peled, Y., and Perzon, S. (2021) 'Systemic Model for Technology Integration in Teaching', *Education and information technologies*, 27(2), pp. 2661–2675.

Pérez-Sanagustin, M., Nussbaum, M., Hilliger, I., Alario-Hoyos, C., Heller, R.S., Twining, P., and Tsai, C. (2017) 'Research on ICT in K-12 Schools – A Review of Experimental and Survey-based Studies in Computers & Education 2011 to 2015', *Computers & Education*, 104 (January 2017), pp. A1–A15.

Sánchez-Prieto, J., Huang, F., Olmos-Miguelanaz, S., Garcia-Penalvo, F., and Teo, T. (2019) 'Exploring the Unknown: The Effect of Resistance to Change and Attachment on Mobile Adoption among Secondary Pre-service Teachers', *British Journal of Educational Technology*, 50(5), pp. 2433.

Selwyn, N. (2018) *Telling Tales on Technology: Qualitative Studies of Technology and Education*. 2nd edn. Oxon: Routledge.

Selwyn, N. et al. (2019) 'What's Next for Ed-Tech? Critical Hopes and Concerns for the 2020s', *Learning, Media and Technology*, 45(1), pp. 1–6.

Spiteri, M., and Chang Rundgren, S. N. (2020) 'Literature Review on the Factors Affecting Primary Teachers' Use of Digital Technology', *Technology, Knowledge and Learning*, 25, pp. 115–128.

Stringer, E., Lewin, C., and Coleman, R. (2019) *Using Digital Technology to Improve Learning*. London: Education Endowment Foundation.

Talip, R., and Tiop, R. (2020) 'The Effect of Educational Organizational Commitment as a Moderator Towards Principal Technology Leadership in Curriculum Management and Teachers' Self-efficacy', *Malaysian Journal of Social Sciences and Humanities*, 5(3), pp. 30–46.

TALIS (2018) *Teaching and Learning International Survey: Insight and Interpretations*. Paris: TALIS.

Tang, Y. (2021) 'Does Information and Communication Technology (ICT) Empower Teacher Innovativeness: A Multilevel, Multisite Analysis', *Education Technology Research Development*, 69, pp. 3009–3028.

Tondeur, J. et al. (2017) 'Understanding the Relationship between Teachers' Pedagogical Beliefs and Technology Use in Education: A Systematic Review of Qualitative Evidence', *Educational Technology Research and Development*, 65(3), pp. 555–575.

Twining, P. (2010) 'Educational Information Technology Research Methodology: looking back and moving forward', in McDougall, A, Murnane, J, Jones, A., and Reynolds, N. (eds.) *Researching IT in Education: Theory, Practice and Future Directions*. London: Routledge, pp. 151–168.

Twining, P. (2018) *Extending Guidance on Qualitative Research*. The halfbaked.education blog. https://halfbaked.education/extending-guidance-on-qualitative-research/

Twining, P. (2019) *From Reflection To Practitioner Research – The Best form of CPD*. The halfbaked.education blog. https://halfbaked.education/from-reflection-to-practitioner-research/

Twining, P., and Aubrey-Smith, F. (2021) *How to Unlock Education Research*. London: SecEd.

Twining, P., Browne, N., et al. (2017a) *NP3: New Purposes, New Practices, New Pedagogy: Meta-analysis Report*. London: Society for Educational Studies. http://edfutures.net/images/e/e7/NP3_Meta-analysis_report.pdf

Twining, P. et al. (2017b) 'Some Guidance on Conducting and Reporting Qualitative Studies', *Computers & Education*, 106, pp. A1–A9.

Twining, P., et al. (2022) 'This is How to Reposition Teachers as Experts'. *EduResearch Matters*. Melbourne: Australian Association for Research in Education. https://www.aare.edu.au/blog/?p=12747

Universities UK (2022) *Higher Education Facts and figures*. London.

University of Melbourne (2022) *Library: Free Online Resources for Teachers*. https://unimelb.libguides.com/c.php?g=402863&p=2741317

Visible Learning (2021) *Meta X*. https://www.visiblelearningmetax.com/

Warioba, M., Machumu, H., Kulunga, K., and Mtweve, L. (2021) 'Adoption of ICT as a Pedagogical Tool in Community Secondary Schools in Tanzania: Possibilities and Constraints', *Education and Information Technologies*, 27(2), pp. 2835–2858.

Zhao, Y. (2018) *Why What Works May Hurt: Side Effects in Education*. New York: Teachers College Press.

CHAPTER

3

What do we mean by effective pedagogy?

Research about the use of digital technology in education consistently tells us that it is not technology itself that has an impact on learning but the way in which digital technology is used (Aubrey-Smith, 2021; Luckin, 2018). Furthermore, when digital technology has been used appropriately to improve teaching and learning, it has been informed by effective pedagogy (Stringer, Lewin et al., 2020).

In this chapter, we explore the term 'effective pedagogy' – by unpacking different definitions of *pedagogy* and *effectiveness* and the many ways in which they are used. We then introduce some particular considerations for teachers when thinking about what effective pedagogy means.

Defining pedagogy

Around the world in education, there is a focus on pedagogy in a way that we have never seen before. The word *pedagogy* is now being used in classrooms, as well as lecture theatres, and in teacher planning, as well as research papers. This is fantastic. It means that in schools, we are collectively focusing on the space that makes the biggest difference in learning.

As a result of this increased focus, there are also some associated problems. Problem one is that there are lots of different definitions of pedagogy (at the time of writing there were just under 92 million pages with definitions according to Google!). Problem two is that pedagogy is currently being used as an umbrella term to refer to many different things (e.g. theories, values, beliefs, methods, practices, approaches, political agendas, etc.). This means that when we have professional conversations about pedagogy, each of us often takes away different perceptions, and, consequently, conclusions about what actions we need to take next.

DOI: 10.4324/9781003321637-3

So what exactly do we mean by pedagogy?

The term *pedagogy* is generally used to refer to the strategies or methods used by teachers in their teaching practices. However, as teaching has become more research-informed, the use of the word *pedagogy* has been increasingly adopted as a general term to incorporate a number of things, including the following:

- Pedagogical Theories
- Pedagogical Beliefs
- Pedagogical Stances
- Pedagogical Intentions
- Pedagogical Approaches
- Pedagogical Methods
- Pedagogical Practices
- Politicised Pedagogy

Given the significance of the role of pedagogy when thinking about digital technology in education (as well as far more widely across education!), it is important to be clear on the distinct definitions that we are using.

Here are terms you need to know:

Pedagogy – this is an umbrella term which incorporates everything that relates to how we support learning. This includes ideas around what teaching means and what the role of a teacher should be, what learning means and what the role of a learner should be, and the nature of knowledge.

Pedagogical theories (or theories of pedagogy) – these are socially accepted explanations about views of teachers and teaching, views of learners and learning, and views of knowledge. The four most important pedagogical theories are Behaviourist theory, Individual Constructivist theory, Social-Constructivist theory, and Sociocultural theory. These theories are generally attributed to or associated with well-known theorists such as Piaget, Vygotsky, Shulman, Skinner, Bourdieu, and Lave and Wenger. Think of these as different explanations about how learners learn. Note that some of the theories we think of as being pedagogical theories were actually theories about learners' development (e.g. Piaget's work) rather than learning per se.

It is important to recognise that a theory is a way of explaining something – either we align with a theory or we do not. You cannot pick and mix parts of different explanations – one explanation is going to fit your world view better than another.

Pedagogical Beliefs (or pedagogical stance) – these are underlying views or beliefs about the purposes or goals of schooling and how learning should be supported. These beliefs usually align with a theory of pedagogy but this may not be known or recognised by the person or group of people holding the pedagogical belief (as that depends on them being aware of the research literature). Pedagogical Beliefs may be **Conscious** (you are aware of them), **Espoused** (e.g. stated and talked about), or **Implicit** (e.g. impacting on Enacted Practice). Pedagogical Stance could be collective (a school's Pedagogical Stance) or individual (a teacher's Pedagogical Stance). Think of these as the big ideas underpinning everything we do to support learning.

For example, a school Teaching and Learning policy will have an embedded set of values and Pedagogical Beliefs which underpin how teaching and learning should take place. These may or may not be explicit (or even defined by those writing the policy). The Pedagogical Beliefs and values may or may not be shared by those who have written the policy, those who are implementing the policy, or those who are being impacted by the policy. This can create gaps or friction between 'intention and reality'. In short – practice will not always match the intentions.

It is important to be aware that we can talk about a set of Pedagogical Beliefs without necessarily believing them (so-called talking the talk). This often happens when we are 'trained' to enact the latest policy or popular trend. Sometimes we think that we believe what we are saying as we have become so familiar with keywords and phrases. However, underneath that, we each have our own set of values and Pedagogical Beliefs that we may or may not be aware of or willing/able to articulate.

Pedagogical intention – this refers to what we plan to do to support learning. Our intentions might be short term (e.g. specific to a moment in time as we respond to a learner) or longer term (e.g. a scheme of work or lesson plan). We implement Pedagogical Practice*s* in order to achieve our Pedagogical Intentions.

Pedagogical Approaches (or Pedagogical Methods) – these are the processes and procedures used to enact particular Pedagogical Beliefs. For example, direct instruction, retrieval practice, interleaving, spaced learning, modelling, call-and-response, and so on. Pedagogical Methods or Approaches can be explicitly taught, repeated, observed, and verified – sometimes becoming adopted as an institutional pedagogy. This is what is most commonly referred to when those working in schools use the term *pedagogy*.

But it's important to be aware that we can use a Pedagogical Approach or Method without necessarily believing in the theory underpinning it. Furthermore, we can use a Pedagogical Method without being aware of the belief system underpinning it and may, in some situations, even disagree with the belief system. This is where it is useful to be mindful of research about communication – and how much of what we communicate to our learners is not through what we do but *how* we do it (Hodges, 2015; Tannen et al., 2015). Our audience will usually be aware if our beliefs do not align with our spoken words or practical actions (even if we are not!).

Pedagogical Practices – these are the things that we do, the practical actions used by anyone involved in supporting learning. These might include *processes* such as using mini whiteboards for whole-class instant response tasks, splitting up the day into 50-minute lessons, enforcing school rules in order to manage learners' behaviour, implementing policies such as on feedback processes or homework requirements, enacting expectations and norms such as what learners should do when they have finished their work or what learners call their teacher, standing at the front of the class introducing a new topic, and communicating using particular vocabulary or body language.

Pedagogical Practices are specific, tangible actions that can be carried out by individuals or groups of people. They are often not explicitly considered nor associated with theories of pedagogy. However, Pedagogical Practices are representations of underpinning values and Pedagogical Beliefs and, as such, are intrinsically value-laden – thus aligning with a theory of pedagogy. When a Pedagogical Practice is being implemented that does not align with your Pedagogical Beliefs this may be counter-productive. For example, if your intention is to use extrinsic rewards, such as star charts, that would not align with a belief that learners' motivation is intrinsic.

Politicised Pedagogy – these are the methods and approaches that we are explicitly or implicitly encouraged to adopt and implement due to policy or political influence (e.g. local, organisational or national). Politicised Pedagogy is often justified by 'policy-led evidence' (rather than evidence-led policy). Descriptions often depend on quantitative-based impact measures (e.g. method x results in an additional y months progress; therefore, we should all use method x).

The relationships between each of these definitions can be seen in Figure 3.1.

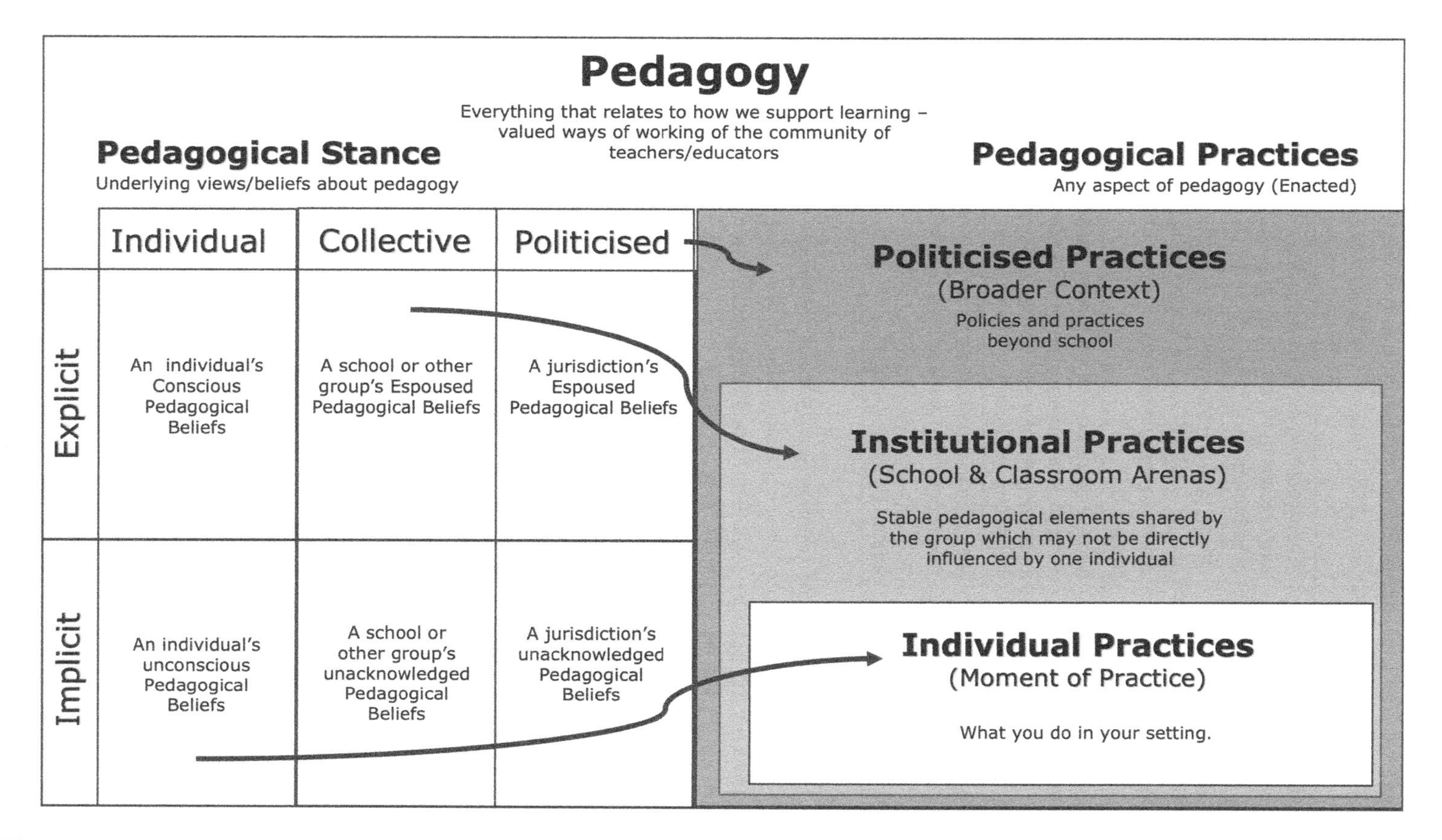

Figure 3.1 Overview of relationships between pedagogical stance and pedagogy

There are many different academic theories explaining how learning happens and therefore how learning should be supported (i.e. pedagogy). Each of the preceding definitions can be seen through the lens of any theory of pedagogy. For example,

Traditional Views on Pedagogy	Where learning involves acquiring information. Learners are extrinsically motivated, and potential for learning is innately determined.
Individual Constructivist Views on Pedagogy	Where learning involves the individual construction of a mental model of reality guided by the teacher. Learners are intrinsically motivated, and learning is limited by age or stage.
Social Constructivist Views on Pedagogy	Where learning involves the co-construction of social reality through interactions with 'more knowledgeable others'. Learners are intrinsically motivated, and learning is not limited by age or stage.
Sociocultural Views on Pedagogy	Where learning involves becoming a member of a community that have shared purposes and valued ways of working. Learners are intrinsically motivated and are not limited by age or stage.

We explore these theories on pedagogy more in the next chapter, but let's just look at why the many different potential definitions of the word *pedagogy* matter so much.

In short, it's because sometimes our Pedagogical Practices are out of alignment with our Pedagogical Beliefs. This may result in mixed messages to our learners and inconsistency in our provision (e.g. Aubrey-Smith, 2022; Aubrey-Smith, 2021).

Contradictory Example 1: 'Same Book, Different Cover'

Having taught from the front of the classroom for many years, a teacher used a wireless device and projection system to perch on a desk at the back of the classroom and teach from there 'so that I am not seen by learners as the sage on the stage'. The teacher's pedagogical intention is to change the power dynamics within the classroom. However, their Pedagogical Practice may be perceived by the learners as still maintaining the same power dynamic – the teacher is still seen as the 'sage on the stage' – they just happen to be at the back of the classroom instead of the front.

Contradictory Example 2: 'Collaboration or Cooperation?'

This teacher believes that learning is enhanced by collaboration being part of lessons (Pedagogical Belief). Thus, they have tasked learners to work in groups of three on shared cloud-based documents, with each learner taking an aspect of their topic, researching it, and writing it up in their section of the shared cloud-based document (Pedagogical Practice). However, the contradiction here is that the teacher has not been encouraging collaboration (which requires learners working together to come to a shared agreement on an output) but cooperation (which results in one product created by splitting up the task so that each learner can work independently on their aspect of it). Thus, there is a mismatch between the teacher's pedagogical belief about the importance of collaboration and their Pedagogical Practice (getting the learners to work cooperatively).

Contradictory Example 3: 'A Pyrrhic Victory'
This teacher believes that learners are intrinsically motivated but uses a point-based competition system to encourage learners to be quicker and work harder on specific tasks or goals. Thus, there is a contradiction between the belief about intrinsic motivation and the use of strategies which rely on extrinsic motivation. Whilst the competition may be effective in the short term, it is likely in the long term to undermine intrinsic motivation (Wilson and Corpus, 2001; Bates, 1979) and, thus, directly oppose their Pedagogical Beliefs.

In all three of these examples, a little more attention to the precise detail about exactly what learners would be doing or experiencing would bring greater clarity. Highlighting inconsistencies makes it more likely that changes in practice will occur – working towards increasing alignment between the teacher's Pedagogical Beliefs and their Pedagogical Practice.

For example, the first teacher could sit with a target intervention group whilst making available a range of resources for other learners to independently use to explore the topic (e.g. through a cloud-based space). Thus, their direct instruction and sequential learning approach is maintained for one group, but the pedagogical approach with the remainder of the class is substantially different.

The second teacher could provide a structure for learners to use to ensure that they collaborate meaningfully in their research – for example, all group members discussing each aspect of the task, commenting on each other's written findings with suggestions for improvements, and/or editing each other's findings to extend the depth of their writing.

The third teacher could reduce the emphasis on external rewards and focus on practices that built on and reinforced the learners' intrinsic motivation, such as providing constructive feedback, focused praise, and, most important, discussion about the inherent value of the task that they are working on.

As you will have seen from the earlier definitions and examples, the word *pedagogy* can mean a great many things. When we use the same word interchangeably to communicate many different meanings, it creates a lack of clarity and a lack of precision in what we do next. This results in confusion and mixed messaging for our learners. This is unhelpful.

Ultimately, we cannot expect to make meaningful change or improvement if we cannot clearly define what we are seeking to change.

It is important that we become much more precise when we use these terms so that as we start to think about effectiveness, improvements, and impact, we know and agree on exactly what we are talking about.

What do we mean by effective pedagogy?

As you will see from the definitions set out earlier, there are some embedded issues with the generic use of the term *effective pedagogy* within research about digital technology. The word *effective* is in itself subjective and is usually considered to refer to being successful in producing a desired or intended result. But what is the result that we are referring to in that phrase 'effective pedagogy'? Do we mean effective pedagogical approaches? Effective Pedagogical Practices? Socially agreed Pedagogical Beliefs? Pedagogy that leads to particular outcomes?

The term *effective* is dependent on the values of the belief system from which it emerges. Thus, one person's view on whether something is effective may be different to another person's view. It is vitally important to be aware, therefore, that what one teacher, leader, researcher, or politician believes is effective pedagogy may be ideologically very different from the views of others. This applies, even within the same nation, the same policy, the same trust, the same school, and even when teaching from the same lesson plan. We know that effective educational provision requires alignment between an educational vision and its policies and practice (Butler et al., 2018) and that systemically, this alignment needs to exist at the national, school, and individual teacher levels (Twining et al., 2021). However, on a smaller scale, the same is true for our Pedagogical Beliefs, Intentions, and Practices – they need to be aligned in order for our own provision to be effective.

All of this becomes rather problematic from a policy and practice perspective because pedagogical discussions in schools and within school-facing material often prioritise particular views of what our Pedagogical Beliefs should be – usually assuming that we should all align with constructivist theories.

A common example of this is the way that most school-facing materials encourage scaffolding and modelling:

> Effective pedagogies involve scaffolding pupil learning.
>
> *(National College for School Leadership, 2012, p. 7)*

> In delivering effective teaching, teachers: plan effective lessons, making good use of modelling, explanations, and scaffolds to support learning.
>
> *(EEF, 2021, p. 13)*

It is highly likely that you will either use the term *scaffolding* yourself or that you have heard others use it in relation to learning. You may or may not be aware that the concept of scaffolding learning is a core part of a Social Constructivist pedagogical stance. This does not make it right or wrong. However, this term does indicate a particular pedagogical position.

Over time, phrases and inferred messages prioritising particular pedagogical stances become embedded in materials setting out what 'good teaching' looks like (Aubrey-Smith, 2021). In turn, this affects the pedagogical approaches that teachers believe are the norm or expected. Judgements become based on the adoption of these institutionalised pedagogical approaches. Consequently, these expectations affect how teachers frame their own teaching in conversation with others (e.g. Becker and Riel, 1999). This creates a culture where professional conversation pivots around an assumption that a particular pedagogical stance is the 'right' one, and attention shifts to evaluating its implementation rather than considering its appropriateness.

You may have noticed that school leaders often talk about 'good pedagogy' or about '*our* pedagogy' – often framed as if teachers adopt leadership views automatically into their own belief system rather than simply replicating observable practices in order to align with expectations and accountability measures (e.g. Coe et al., 2020; Husbands and Pearce, 2012). Yet, from a Sociocultural perspective, pedagogy cannot exist without those who engage with it. As one of the leading thinkers in this space, Alexander (2009) argues, by nature of there being many who engage, there are multiple interpretations of what pedagogy consequently looks like in practice. Thus, it is problematic to consider any pedagogy itself in absolute terms because there will be multiple versions of pedagogy rather than one single 'right' version.

Consequently, there cannot be a single 'right version' of *effective* pedagogy.

This presents a problem with the terminology across the literature, where findings often relate to what is valued within pedagogy – the approaches or acts of practice – rather than the values or belief systems on which pedagogy itself is founded (Coe et al., 2014). This perpetuates a focus on surface-level practices rather than underlying beliefs and values.

Given that evidence suggests that what we believe, what we say, and what we do, do not always perfectly align or reflect each other (e.g. Cooper and Olson, 1996), a focus on surface-level practice seems problematic.

Thus, in discussions about refining, changing, or improving practice, there is a central problem. How can we make meaningful changes to our practice without understanding the belief systems that such changes are built on? Perhaps sometimes we are at risk of just swapping one recommended teaching strategy for another recommended teaching strategy.

You may be familiar with the expression 'the grass is always greener', whereby we see the appeal of something different precisely because it is different. Sometimes this happens when we hear about new research or innovative strategies for classroom practice – we assume that newer, alternative ideas will be better than our current practice and we rush to adopt them. Yet perhaps the grass is not necessarily greener but instead reflects what lies beneath that particular soil – it may not be either better or worse but just different. Similarly, the most effective teaching strategies are not necessarily better strategies. Instead, effective strategies are the ones that are in alignment with the Pedagogical Beliefs of the person leading that classroom. This makes both the strategy and the person leading it more effective and creates professional satisfaction – resulting in effective pedagogy and individual efficacy (Bandura, 1977).

It is helpful to highlight here that being effective is not synonymous with being 'good'. Being 'effective' simply means that our practices are aligning with our values and beliefs. History reminds us of people who have been very effective at achieving unjust or immoral outcomes. As teachers, we must take time to understand what our values and beliefs suggest that 'good' means and then looks like in practice.

It is also helpful to be aware that when we are with our learners and under some kind of pressure – perhaps feeling unwell or overwhelmed, responding to a behavioural situation, or running out of time – we tend to revert to strategies and actions which are familiar to us in order to reduce our own cognitive load (Sweller, 1988). Those familiar strategies or actions may not be effective (or even desirable) and may enhance any conflict between our beliefs and practice.

If we do not align our Pedagogical Beliefs and the changes that we make to our classroom practice, then surface-level changes (e.g. teaching strategies) are the equivalent of just moving from one grassy green field to another. There has been change, but if there is a lack of alignment between our Pedagogical Beliefs and Pedagogical Practices, then it is unlikely that the change will be optimally effective. We often fall into this by accident by adhering to recommendations or trends (including Politicised Pedagogy or organisational pedagogical approaches). Darvin and Norton (2015) talk about agents (in this case teachers) acting within a spectrum of consent and dissent – where we can be observed to do or not do things that we have been encouraged to do by those who influence our thinking. However, what appears to be consent (e.g. adhering to trends or expectations) may sometimes simply be a matter of dominant practice, in other words performing actions without necessarily subscribing to the Pedagogical Beliefs that underpin them. We also need to be aware that a teacher's *Conscious Beliefs* (what we think we believe) cannot be assumed to represent their *Implicit Beliefs* (what we really believe). We explore this in more detail in Chapter 4.

As teachers, we face many influences and pressures. These come from our colleagues, leaders, and managers; students and their families; the media; the community; and accountability structures. It is little wonder that these affect what we say, intend to do, and enact in our practice. Research by Goe, Bell, and Little (2008) and Coe et al. (2014) found that what teachers say to others about teaching and learning is heavily influenced by social desirability bias – an aim to please others. As Buchanan (2015) argues, in a school environment with a high public accountability agenda, this can be particularly problematic. This is because social desirability bias embeds itself into the accepted voice of the teacher even if it does not necessarily represent their personal views. In other words, the teacher (probably largely subconsciously) begins to reflect an orchestrated voice back to the people around them.

In an environment where we are thinking about digital technology, it is helpful to consider that this may not just apply to teachers. Hattie and Hamilton (2020) argue that this also applies to digital technology suppliers who are designing, developing, and supporting the implementation of products for school use – developing a well-intentioned echo chamber of what 'best use' might look like.

However, teaching is a profession, and like any other profession, professionals are those who understand what they do and also why they do it – taking into account the great many influences shaping and affecting them (Hargreaves, 2000; Hargreaves & Fullan, 2020).

For the education community – of peers, leaders, and those in supporting roles – this means that supporting meaningful professional practice and development has become more complex.

What does this mean in relation to digital technology?

When unpacking what we mean by using digital technology effectively, we need to consider the different trends and embedded bias within academic literature, policy agendas, and social interactions as set out earlier. In other words, how we respond to digital technology and how digital technology responds to us (Orlikowski and Scott, 2008). It is helpful to remember that as teachers, our relationship with digital technology is not just about how we use it (or do not use it) in school. We also experience digital technology and are affected by it in many beyond-school parts of our lives, and this all affects how we interpret the role and relevance of digital technology. In Chapter 5, we explore the many influences that affect how we think about digital technology in relation to our professional practice. It is helpful to keep in mind that every person involved in bringing digital technology to the learner will have their own set of influences, assumptions, social desirability biases, and ideological aspirations. This shapes us all – policy influencers and makers, budget holders and infrastructure gatekeepers, product designers and developers, school leaders and teachers, families and learners.

In addition, research tells us that teachers' Pedagogical Beliefs often align with their chosen subject or area of expertise (e.g. Karaseva et al., 2015; John, 2005) or existing learning dispositions (Perry and Ball, 2004). In other words, a maths specialist is likely to hold different views on pedagogy than a science or music specialist. These trends will also apply to policy shapers and decision-makers, product designers and developers, and school leaders. We will all perceive there to be a 'best' version of pedagogy based on our deeply seated personal value system. This may or may not align with the views of colleagues in our phase or department, school, or wider organisation.

This makes a difference to teachers' uses of digital technology. For example, Karaseva et al. (2015) found that teachers in different subject specialisms had views on digital technology use which were far more aligned with each other than with those of staff in other subject areas. Teachers shared some views on what effective pedagogy looked like but only within their specific subject domain. As Selwyn and Kelchtermans (2020) point out, teaching behaviour is mainly driven by interests which are not necessarily specific to teaching. These can form prior to, during, or after pre-service teacher education and can continue throughout a teacher's professional life in response to many other influences (Webster et al., 2012). Thus, a teacher's choice of career, school, subject, or phase suggests an alignment with their pre-existing internalised identity (Moore Johnson and Birkeland, 2003). We are 'drawn' to teach particular subjects or age ranges. All these factors affect (a) a teacher's pedagogical stance, (b) a teacher's relationship with digital technology, and, thus, (c) the relationship of a teacher's pedagogical stance with their use of digital technology in teaching practice.

There has been a great deal of research concerned with conceptualising the ways in which learning experiences are impacted by the presence of digital technology in teaching practices (Buchanan, 2020). Fawns (2022) argues that digital technology and pedagogy are so entangled that we can no longer see them as two separate considerations, which has implications not just for learning and teaching but also for leadership and management (Weatherby and Clark-Wilson, 2019).

There are two important messages to draw out of this.

First, it is the teacher's Pedagogical Stance which shapes *how* digital technology is used or not used. Second, the way that a teacher incorporates digital technology into learning amplifies the teacher's underlying Pedagogical Beliefs – whether they are aware of that or not (Aubrey-Smith, 2021; Twining et al., 2017).

However, there is an important but very subtle detail within this. It is entirely possible for a teacher to adopt digital technology and use it based on instruction from a third party (e.g. a colleague, leader, EdTech champion, or professional network). Many teachers use online and offline networks and resources to source ideas recommended by other teachers – often preferring suggestions that can be immediately replicated (e.g. 'best-practice ideas'). What we need to be aware of is that those ideas have emerged from a particular set of Pedagogical Beliefs and values held by the person who created or defined that idea. They may or may not align with our own. Therefore, the 'idea' (which may be a Pedagogical Approach or a Pedagogical Practice) may or may not align with our own Pedagogical Beliefs, even if the action itself is appealing, achievable, and actionable. This creates a very subtle friction within our classroom practice. In turn, this can send mixed messages to our learners about the core features of pedagogy (i.e. views on learners and learning, views on teachers and teaching, views on knowledge). So it is possible to use digital technology in ways that do not align with our personal Pedagogical Beliefs, but doing so will cause some problems – as illustrated with the 'contradictory examples' earlier in this chapter.

Therefore, to be meaningful, the phrase 'effective pedagogy' must take account of (a) how the actions that our learners experience align with or contradict the underlying beliefs and values from which they have emerged and (b) our own Pedagogical Beliefs. If our learners are experiencing and internalising the pedagogy that our beliefs suggest we want them to experience, then we can consider our individual pedagogy to be effective.

However, if our actions are not in alignment with our personal Pedagogical Beliefs, then our learners will be receiving very mixed messages from us. These will be seen through our explicit actions as well as our implicit communication (e.g. embedded bias within our vocabulary, our body language, the way that we pace and motivate, the in situ decisions that we make within our practice, and so forth). These are subtle (and often subconscious) but fundamentally very powerful messages that reflect our views of learners and learning, our views of teachers and teaching, and our views of knowledge.

For example, we might focus on enhancing test performance by assigning past papers to our learners and scheduling regular test practice. In parallel to this, we may share our frustrations with colleagues about a system which prioritises testing. These two things can coexist in parallel at the same time yet represent opposing Pedagogical Beliefs. The reason that this becomes problematic is because our learners will be aware of the contradictions even if we don't explicitly discuss them with our class. For example, what messages do we convey about testing through the level of enthusiasm with which we introduce test papers? Are we inferring real-world value? Or are we inferring a task with little benefit for the learner? What kinds of vocabulary do we use when discussing test questions and test outcomes with our learners? Are we inferring an opportunity to develop real-world skills and techniques or are we inferring a benefit-free process? Both ways of thinking about tests within existing systems are possible – they just represent different underlying Pedagogical Beliefs. However, the problematic part is that what we say and what we do may not align. Our learners are more likely to internalise implied lack of *value* than they are to value the benefits of *rehearsal*. Therefore, the misalignment causes not just confusion but also fundamentally undermines both the Pedagogical Practice and the projected belief. This creates ineffective pedagogy.

Detail matters because it is not 'what' is taking place which learners will internalise; it is 'how' it is taking place. It is the alignment between a practice and a belief that leads to effective pedagogy and the misalignment that leads to ineffective pedagogy. This is at the heart of why 'effective pedagogy' cannot be seen as something that can be scaled, replicated, or transferrable in isolation from the Pedagogical Beliefs of those who will be enacting it.

Conclusion

In the previous section, we introduced issues which lead to effective or ineffective pedagogy framed around an individual teacher. However, pedagogy is often discussed as externalised – belonging to a group rather than a person. This is problematic because there is little consensus globally or nationally in political, academic, or social domains about what effective pedagogy means. In part, this is due to a lack of precision and clarity by the individuals within such groups, and in part, it is because unanimous agreement would be highly unlikely given the subjective values and belief systems which underpin pedagogical views.

As set out earlier, whilst many schools have an established Teaching and Learning Strategy, there is still evidence to suggest notable variance between teachers in any given school – typically seeing a mix of Traditional, Constructivist, and Sociocultural stances even within a high-performing school (TPEA, 2022). We need to ask ourselves – to what extent are our individual classrooms and our wider organisations presenting a *consistent* message about what it means to learn and to be a learner, what role other people play in supporting learning, what we mean by knowledge, and what the role of school should be.

If learners are not experiencing consistency in our messages about what it means to learn, then we are creating, and not resolving, confusion for our learners.

However, asking teachers about their pedagogical stance can create challenges. This is partly because as teachers we rarely talk about our pedagogical stance (Ertmer, 2010; Tondeur et al., 2017), and when pedagogy is discussed in school, it tends to be treated as 'rules for practice' (Husu and Tirri, 2007). This affects what we say and how we act as we seek to align with those perceived rules (Taber, 2011). This is partly because consideration of individual teacher's underlying beliefs has historically not been a regular focus of conversation in most schools. That needs to change.

We need to encourage more frequent and more precise conversations about exactly what we mean when we talk about effective pedagogy, and in order to contribute meaningfully to that discussion, we need to start by unpacking our own individual Pedagogical Beliefs.

References

Alexander, R. (2009) 'Towards a Comparative Pedagogy', in Cowen, R. and Kazamias, A. M. (eds.) *International Handbook of Comparative Education*. London: Springer, pp. 923–942.

Aubrey-Smith, F. (2021) *An exploration of the relationship between teachers pedagogical stance and their use of ICT in classroom practice*. Doctoral Thesis. The Open University.

Aubrey-Smith, F. (2022) Intentions v Reality: What's Really Going on for Our Learners When We Use EdTech? *Report for the Technology, Pedagogy and Education Association Research and Development Grant 2021*.

Bandura, A. (1977) 'Self-Efficacy: Toward a Unifying Theory of Behavioral Change', *Psychological Review*, 84(2), pp. 191–215.

Bates, J. A. (1979) 'Extrinsic Reward and Intrinsic Motivation: A Review with Implications for the Classroom', *Review of Educational Research*, 49(4), pp. 557–576.

Becker, H. J., and Riel, M. M. (1999) 'Teacher Professionalism and the Emergence of Constructivist-Compatible Pedagogies'. Paper presented at meeting of *American Educational Research Association*, Montreal.

Buchanan, R. (2015) 'Teacher Identity and Agency in an Era of Accountability', *Teachers and Teaching: Theory and Practice*, 21(6), pp. 700–719.

Buchanan, R., (2020) 'Through Growth to Achievement: Examining Edtech as a Solution to Australia's Declining Educational Achievement'. *Policy Futures in Education*, 18(8), pp. 1026–1043.

Butler, D., Leahy, M., Twining, P., Akoh, B., Chtouki, Y., Farshadnia, S., Moore, K., Nikolov, R., Pascual, C., Sherman, B., and Valtonen, T. (2018) 'Education Systems in the Digital Age: The Need for Alignment', *Technology, Knowledge and Learning*, 23, pp. 473–494.

Coe, R. et al. (2014) *What Makes Great Teaching? Review of the Underpinning Research*. Durham: Center for Evaluation and Monitoring, Durham University and The Sutton Trust.

Coe, R. et al. (2020) *Evidence Review Great Teaching Toolkit*. Cambridge: Evidence Based Education.

Cooper, K., and Olson, M. R. (1996) 'The Multiple "I's" of Teacher Identity', in Kompf, M. et al. (eds.) *Changing Research and Practice: Teachers' Professionalism, Identities and Knowledge*. London: Falmer Press, pp. 78–89.

Darvin, R., and Norton, B. (2015) 'Identity and a Model of Investment in Applied Linguistics', *Annual Review of Applied Linguistics*, 35, pp. 36–56.

Education Endowment Foundation (2021) *Teacher Feedback to improve Pupil Learning*. London: EEF.

Ertmer, P. A., and Ottenbreit Leftwich, A. (2010) 'Teacher Technology Change: How Knowledge, Confidence, Beliefs, and Culture Intersect', *Journal of Research on Technology in Education*, 42(3), pp. 255–284.

Fawns, T. (2022) 'An Entangled Pedagogy: Looking Beyond the Pedagogy – Technology Dichotomy', *Postdigital Science and Education*, 4(3), pp. 711–728.

Goe, L., Bell, C., and Little, O. (2008) *Approaches to Evaluating Teacher Effectiveness: A Research Synthesis*. Washington, DC: National Comprehensive Center for Teacher Quality.

Hargreaves, A. (2000) 'Four Ages of Professionalism and Professional Learning', *Teachers and Teaching: History and Practice*, 6(2), pp. 151–182.

Hargreaves, A., and Fullan, M. (2020) 'Professional Capital after the Pandemic: Revisiting and Revising Classic Understandings of Teachers' Work', *Journal of Professional Capital and Community*, 5(3–4), pp. 327–336.

Hattie, J., and Hamilton, A. (2020) *Why We Focus on the Wrong Drivers in Education*. London: Sage Publications Ltd.

Hodges, A. (2015) 'Intertextuality in Discourse', in Tannen, D., Hamilton, H. E., and Schiffrin, D. (eds.) *The Handbook of Discourse Analysis*. 2nd edn. US: Wiley-Blackwell.

Husbands, C., and Pearce, J. (2012) *What Makes Great Pedagogy? Nine Claims from Research*. London: National College for Teaching and Leadership.

Husu, J., and Tirri, K. (2007) 'Developing Whole School Pedagogical Values-A Case of Going through the Ethos of "Good Schooling"', *Teaching and Teacher Education*, 23(4), pp. 390–401.

John, P. (2005) 'The Sacred and the Profane: Subject Sub-culture, Pedagogical Practice and Teachers' Perceptions of the Classroom Uses of ICT', *Educational Review*, 57(4), pp. 471–490.

Karaseva, A., Siibak, A., and Pruulmann-Vengerfeldt, P. (2015) 'Relationships between Teachers' Pedagogical Beliefs, Subject Cultures, and Mediation Practices Of Students' Use of Digital Technology', *Cyberpsychology*, 9(1). Article 6.

Luckin, R. (2018) *Enhancing Learning and Teaching with Technology: What the Research Says*. London: UCL Institute of Education Press.

Moore Johnson, S., and Birkeland, S. (2003) 'The Schools That Teachers Choose', *Educational Leadership*, 60(8), pp. 20–24.

National College for School Leadership (2012) *What Makes Great Pedagogy? Nine Claims from Research*. London: National College for School Leadership.

Orlikowski, W., and Scott, S. (2008) 'Sociomateriality: Challenging the Separation of Technology, Work and Organization', *Academy of Management Annals*, 2(1), pp. 433–474.

Perry, C., and Ball, I. (2004) 'Teacher Subject Specialisms and their Relationships to Learning Styles, Psychological Types and Multiple Intelligences: Implications for Course Development', *Teacher Development*, 8(1), pp. 9–28.

Selwyn, N., and Kelchtermans, G. (2020) "The Micropolitics of Educational Work", Meet the Education Researcher. Podcast 27 January 2020. https://podcast.app/meet-the-education-researcher-p339917/

Stringer, E., Lewin, C., and Coleman, R. (2020) *Using Digital Technology to Improve Learning*. London: Educational Endowment Foundation.

Sweller, J. (1988) 'Cognitive Load during Problem Solving: Effects on Learning', *Cognitive Science*, 12, pp. 257–285.

Taber, K. S. (2011) 'Constructivism as Educational Theory: Contingency in Learning, and Optimally Guided Instruction', in Hassaskhah, J. (ed.) *Educational Theory*. New York: Nova Science Publishers Inc., pp. 39–61.

Tannen, D. et al. (2015) *The Handbook of Discourse Analysis*. 2nd edn. Chichester: Blackwell.

Tondeur, J. et al. (2017) "Understanding the Relationship between Teachers' Pedagogical Beliefs and Technology Use in Education: A Systematic Review of Qualitative Evidence', *Educational Technology Research and Development*, 65(3), pp. 555–575.

TPEA (2022) 'Intentions v Reality: What's Really Going on for Our Learners When We Use EdTech?' Report for Technology, Pedagogy and Education Association.

Twining, P., Browne, N., et al. (2017) *NP3: New Purposes, New Practices, New Pedagogy: Meta-analysis Report*. London: Society for Educational Studies. http://edfutures.net/images/e/e7/NP3_Meta-analysis_report.pdf

Twining, P., Butler, D., Fisser, P., Leahy, M., Shelton, C., Forget-Dubois, N., and Lacasse, M. (2021) 'Developing a Quality Curriculum in a Technological Era', *Education Technology Research Development*, 69(4), pp. 2285–2308. https://link.springer.com/article/10.1007/s11423-020-09857-3

Weatherby, K., and Clark-Wilson, A. (2019) 'Getting inside the Black Box: Piloting and Evaluating Education Technology in Schools', *Impact: Journal of the Chartered College of Teaching*, 5, pp. 23–25.

Webster, A. et al. (2012) *What Influences Teachers to Change Their Practice? A Rapid Research Review*. Bristol: Centre for Understanding Behaviour Change.

Wilson, L., and Corpus, D. (2001) 'The Effects of Reward Systems on Academic Performance', *Middle School Journal*, 33(1), pp. 56–60.

CHAPTER

4

How do I learn about my own pedagogical beliefs?

In the last chapter, we explored what is meant by the word *pedagogy* and unpacked definitions of different aspects of pedagogy. This chapter takes you through a guided activity which will help you more forensically understand your own Pedagogical Beliefs.

As Patricia Murphy set out in her innovative pedagogy framework (Twining et al., 2017), ultimately, pedagogy is about surfacing what we mean across four distinct dimensions:

- Views of learners and learning
- Views of teachers and teaching
- Views of knowledge
- Views of the purpose (or goals) of schooling

We tend to think about our own pedagogy in relation to approaches and practices (Teaching and Learning Strategies and associated actions). We think far less often about our embedded values and beliefs and the implicit way that these are communicated to others through our body language, prioritisation, tone, and relationships. This chapter encourages you to think about aspects of pedagogy that we may not usually talk about in explicit terms.

First, we introduce you to four teacher personas by describing typical Pedagogical Practice for each one. When you read each of these, you may recognise your own practice or things that you have seen colleagues do. Later, we guide you through a sequence of activities that will support you to explicitly surface your own Pedagogical Beliefs. This will help you reflect on your beliefs in detail and surface aspects that you may not have previously considered. Finally, we explain the theory behind these illustrations and activities.

DOI: 10.4324/9781003321637-4

Guided Activity 4.1: Surfacing your pedagogical beliefs

Purpose: To surface your personal pedagogical beliefs.
Time needed: 20 minutes

We strongly recommend you use the editable version of this Guided Activity, which you can download from www.onelifelearning.co.uk/resources

Let's start by introducing you to four different teacher personas, Niq, Sam, Aba, and Jo. These teachers could be located in any school, working with learners of any age. The teachers could be at any stage of their career and could be any gender or from any cultural background.

As you read each illustration:

1) Highlight phrases or words within each of the examples that reflect the kinds of Pedagogical Practices that you have enacted.
2) Consider what each example reveals about the four dimensions of pedagogy (views of learners and learning, views of teachers and teaching, views of knowledge, and views of the purpose [or goals] of schooling).

Niq's typical pedagogical practice

Niq's classroom is organised with the learners' tables in rows facing the front of the class. Niq uses a seating plan which places learners with special educational needs (including behavioural needs) at the front of the classroom, and learners whom Niq trusts to conform with expectations in rows at the back. Niq will typically introduce a topic on the board at the front of the classroom. Niq will have carefully planned a learning sequence that breaks the topic down into small pieces that are introduced sequentially, one at a time. Niq will ask closed questions to check that the learners are following what is being said. After the input, which lasts approximately 35% of the lesson time, Niq gives the learners activities to do which involve applying what has been taught to reinforce it and check that they have understood it. Niq has carefully prepared different activities for different groups of learners who are perceived to be of different abilities. This is in order to differentiate the task so that it is appropriate for the differing ability levels of learners. Learners are grouped by ability and carry out assigned tasks and, then depending on their score, progress on to predefined 'next step' tasks. Different ability groups are given different worksheets on which they record their responses. Learners work individually, they are discouraged from talking to each other as this is distracting for the rest of the class. Niq sits at the front of the class responding to requests for help or circulates around to check how learners are progressing. At the end of the lesson,

Niq gives a quick recap of the key points for the learners to remember before collecting their work, which will be marked and returned in the follow-on lesson.

Sam's typical pedagogical practice

Sam's classroom has clusters of tables organised into horseshoe shapes where learners are all oriented towards the front of the classroom. Learners are allocated to a table, based on their current level of competence. Sam usually starts the lesson with teacher input and checks the learners' understanding at regular intervals. Once Sam feels that the majority of the class have understood the main points, each group is given an activity to do to reinforce the teaching input. Learners are encouraged to cooperate with each other, talking about the task, and each learner completes their own response. Sam tends to work with one group whilst keeping an overview of what the other learners are doing. Sam tries to elicit any misconceptions that the learners in the group have – and then helps correct those misconceptions. At the end of the lesson, Sam reinforces the key points for the learners to understand, using examples of their misconceptions as part of checking their understanding.

Aba's typical pedagogical practice

Aba's classroom has groups of tables. Learners are not ability grouped. Aba typically starts their time with learners by providing teacher input, regularly asks questions, and encourages the learners to discuss the answers in pairs before responding. Once Aba feels that the majority of the class have understood the main points, they are given an activity to do in their groups. The learners are expected to collaborate to develop one shared group response to the activity. Aba circulates, talking with groups and ensuring that everyone is contributing to the group discussions. The learners know that towards the end of their time with the teacher, one of the groups will be asked to share their work with the rest of the class.

Jo's typical pedagogical practice

Jo's classroom is set up so that it can be re-organised to suit the activities that are taking place. The approach is generally problem-based. Individual learners may be focused on different problems that are of particular interest to them personally. These are often linked to their local community. Investigating a problem and deciding how to address it might take weeks to complete and involve interdisciplinary work. Learners are expected to work individually or in self-selected teams and can choose how they are going to approach their problem.

At the start of each day, Jo leads a whole-class session to sort out organisational issues and hear from individuals and teams about how their work is progressing and discuss any issues that they need help with. Jo encourages learners to talk to each other about the full range of ideas in that shared space – exploring themes and patterns and posing their own consequent questions. This may involve learners sharing what they are working on. Jo asks open questions and encourages learners to capture their ideas, review contributions by others, and extend or build on each other's ideas.

Following the whole-class discussion at the start of the day, individuals and teams then carry on with their work. Jo works alongside learners, sometimes providing direct instruction, sometimes modelling how to approach a task, sometimes learning in conjunction with them. How the learners work, the tools and competencies that they use, and the outcomes that they aim to achieve reflect the issue or problem that they are addressing in the context of the community involved. Part of Jo's role is to help the learners understand how different communities operate, and what are seen as appropriate and valued ways of working within those communities. Often Jo is learning from or alongside the learners.

Learners know that their problem-based projects will culminate in a presentation that aims to summarise what they have learnt. These presentations will be shared with a range of audiences beyond the school. The intention is that their work will have an impact – this might be in highlighting an issue or stimulating action to address it or some other tangible outcome.

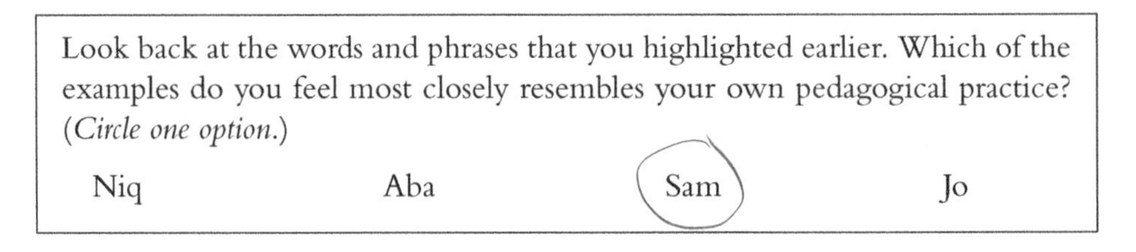

Look back at the words and phrases that you highlighted earlier. Which of the examples do you feel most closely resembles your own pedagogical practice? (*Circle one option.*)

Niq Aba Sam Jo

Having considered these examples and how they align with your own Pedagogical Practice, we are now going to unpack Pedagogical Beliefs in more detail.

Guided Activity 4.2: Understanding your pedagogical alignment

Purpose: To consider, and then identify, which pedagogical stance you feel that you most align with.

Time Needed: 20 minutes

- Step 1: Your typical Pedagogical Practice
- Step 2: Thinking about Learners and Learning
- Step 3: Thinking about Teachers and Teaching
- Step 4: Thinking about knowledge

- Step 5: Thinking about the Purpose of Schooling
- Step 6: Thinking about your overall pedagogical stance
- Step 7: Unpacking pedagogical stances

> We strongly recommend you use the editable version of this Guided Activity, which you can download from www.onelifelearning.co.uk/resources

In this guided activity, Step 1 asks you to reflect on your own teaching by writing a description of your typical Pedagogical Practice. Steps 2–5 each present you with four statements and ask you to think about which of the statements most closely aligns with your personal beliefs. This is intended to help structure your thinking about different dimensions of pedagogy. You will find this process much easier if you have already completed Step 1 before moving on to read Steps 2–5.

You will get the most out of Steps 2–5 if you think carefully about your personal beliefs rather than the words and phrases that you are encouraged to use within your professional conversations. Often we can use socially accepted phrases yet believe something slightly different (Hamachek, 1999), which can distort our self-perception.

Step 1: Your typical pedagogical practice

Write a persona for yourself, which describes your typical Pedagogical Practice. Use the four examples from earlier as a sort of template – make sure you include a description of the layout of your classroom and how learners are organised, as well as describe the key aspects of what you and the learners do.

> My typical Pedagogical Practice …

Before we continue, it is important to bear in mind that Pedagogical Beliefs emerge from deeply rooted personal values and beliefs (we explore this more in Chapter 5). This means that each of us will have deeply seated beliefs which may or may not align with those of colleagues. That's okay!

We are all human beings who bring different experiences and perspectives into our professional environments. What we need to do is to surface these so that we are aware of the impact that these beliefs have on our practice.

Step 2: Thinking about learners and learning

Let's start by thinking about beliefs about what it means to be a learner and what it means to learn. Four statements follow – read them carefully and think about which **one** most closely aligns with what you believe about learning and learners. Remember, there is no right or wrong, there is no hierarchy, and this is not a 'pick and mix' – these reflect four distinct theories about learning and we are looking to see which is the 'best fit' with your own beliefs. This is not about what you currently do but what you believe deep down about learners and learning.

As you work through Steps 2–5, it is important to bear in mind that you are looking for 'best fit' alignment. Different pedagogical stances are underpinned by different theories. If you have two theories (explanations) of the *same phenomenon* (e.g. how people learn), then they cannot both be correct – one of them is going to be a better explanation than the other. Therefore, you should choose only one response in each step.

Put a cross against the **one** that best fits your personal beliefs about learners and learning.

1) Learning is about the active construction of our individual mental model of the world. We each have characteristics (such as age/stage or prior attainment) which constrain what we can learn. Our learning is intrinsically motivated by trying to make sense of the world around us and remove conflicts within our mental model.	
2) Learning is about remembering knowledge. When we learn, we individually acquire and then retrieve knowledge. We each have genetic predispositions which determine our learning potential. Our learning is extrinsically motivated by our desire to meet expectations and work towards rewards or publicly recognised outcomes.	
3) Learning is about actively developing our identity (becoming) as we participate with others who have shared goals and shared valued ways of working (belonging). Our learning is intrinsically motivated by the desire to belong to particular communities and become competent in socially valued activities within those communities.	
4) Learning is about actively constructing knowledge as we are introduced to it through dialogue, particularly with more knowledgeable others. We each have a set of prior experiences which form a base on which we can extend our knowledge. Our learning is intrinsically motivated by trying to make sense of how others in society have constructed ways of seeing and understanding the world.	

Having decided which one of the four descriptions aligns most closely with your beliefs about learning and learners, think about an example of your own everyday practice that reflects the beliefs that you have put a cross against. This might be something that you intend or would like to be able to do or something that you have already done. The process of identifying a tangible example will help you refine your thinking about the precise detail of your beliefs in action. Add the example into the box provided and then identify up to three things that this process has caused you to reflect on.

An example of what this might look like in my own practice is:	
This has caused me to reflect upon the following things:	

Step 3: Thinking about teachers and teaching

As before, choose **one** of the four statements that most closely aligns with your beliefs about teachers and teaching. Again, this is not necessarily about your current practice but about what you deeply believe about teachers and teaching.

1) Teachers provide an environment that supports learners who direct their own learning, with guidance from the teacher to help them develop their individual mental models. Teaching involves providing activities through which learning will occur. For younger children, these activities need to involve physical interaction and concrete experiences. Older learners can extend their mental models through problem-solving and abstraction.	
2) Teachers create learning opportunities that emerge from learners' characteristics and interests. They attempt to make clear connections between school activities and valued ways of working in the world. Teachers encourage shared meaning to emerge from activity in the classroom and make these meanings explicit so that they can be understood and made use of by all the learners.	

3) Teachers have the knowledge their learners need to acquire. They break this down into small steps that need to be learnt in sequence. Drill and practice are used in order for learners to retain knowledge. Pace and competitiveness (e.g. quiz scores, personal best times, competitions) are used to maintain learners' motivation.	
4) Teachers direct learning through scaffolded activities and dialogue. Teaching is seen as providing the opportunity for learners to work with more knowledgeable others. Within their zone of proximal development, learners co-construct their understanding of established subject knowledge claims through interaction.	

Now think about an example of your own everyday practice that reflects the beliefs that you have put a cross against – this might be something that you intend to do or would like to do or something that you have already done. The process of identifying a tangible example will help you refine your thinking about the precise detail of your beliefs in action. Add the example into the box provided and then identify up to three things that this process has caused you to reflect on.

An example of what this might look like in my own practice is:	
This has caused me to reflect upon the following things:	

Step 4: Thinking about knowledge

As before, choose **one** of the four statements that most closely aligns with your beliefs about knowledge.

1) Knowledge consists of objective facts that can be learned, retained, and remembered for later application. Knowledge is independent of context and is represented by symbols such as words or numbers. Knowledge is explicit and held by individuals.	
2) Knowledge is socially constructed; it is a co-constructed mental model of aspects of the world. Individuals acquire knowledge through dialogue, which creates meaning and shared understandings.	
3) Knowledge is individually constructed and is that individual's mental model of the world. Knowledge can be abstracted and transferred across contexts. Knowledge can be used effectively if it fits the individual's own experience.	
4) Knowledge is the ability to act in valued ways in particular contexts. Knowledge can be explicit or tacit.	

Now think about an example of your own everyday practice that reflects these beliefs – this might be something that you intend to do or would like to do or something that you have already done. The process of identifying a tangible example will help you refine your thinking about the precise detail of your beliefs in action. Add the example into the box provided and then identify up to three things that this process has caused you to reflect on.

An example of what this might look like in my own practice is:	
This has caused me to reflect on the following things:	

Step 5: Thinking about the purpose of schooling

As before, choose **one** of the four statements that most closely aligns with your beliefs about what the purposes and goals of schooling should be.

1) Schools should aim to help learners develop their identity through becoming competent members of specific communities who have developed shared understandings of what is valued within those communities and how to be productive within them.	
2) Schools should aim to guide learners so that they develop their mental models and can apply them across contexts.	
3) Schools should aim to scaffold learners in developing their mental models of subject domains and how they are socially constructed so that their mental models can be used across contexts.	
4) Schools should aim to develop learners' knowledge.	

Now think about an example of your own everyday practice that reflects these beliefs that you have put a cross against in the box – this might be something that you intend to do or would like to do or something that you have already done. The process of identifying a tangible example will help you refine your thinking about the precise detail of your beliefs in action. Add the example into the box provided and then identify up to three things that this process has caused you to reflect on.

Write down your view of what the aims of school should be:	
This has caused me to reflect on the following things:	

Step 6: Thinking about your overall pedagogical stance

Through the activities above we invited you to think about a 'best fit' statement for your views on each of the following four themes:

- Views of learners and learning
- Views of teachers and teaching
- Views of knowledge
- Views of the purpose (or goals) of schooling

Each of the best-fit statements aligned with a particular Pedagogical Stance. These were intentionally not in any consistent order. This grid shows you which statement aligned with which pedagogical stance for Steps 2–5.

	Statement 1	**Statement 2**	**Statement 3**	**Statement 4**
Step 2	Individual Constructivist	Traditional	Sociocultural	Social Constructivist
Step 3	Individual Constructivist	Sociocultural	Traditional	Social Constructivist
Step 4	Traditional	Social Constructivist	Individual Constructivist	Sociocultural
Step 5	Sociocultural	Individual Constructivist	Social Constructivist	Traditional

Highlight which statement you aligned with for each step in the table above.

Are your views consistent across the different activities? If not, this might suggest some inconsistency in your thinking about pedagogy, and you may wish to review any that appear to be 'outliers'. This is because a theory is an explanation of a particular way of thinking about something. Different theories provide different explanations, so it is contradictory to believe part of one and part of another. It is more likely that we need to think more deeply about what we really believe.

Look at which pedagogical stance or stances you have highlighted for the steps earlier. Which pedagogical stance does this suggest that your views most closely align with overall? (Circle one)

Traditional | Individual Constructivist | Social Constructivist | Sociocultural

It's important to remember that for the purposes of this task, there is no right or wrong outcome.

Each of us will align with different views on pedagogy, and that's okay! The important outcome is that you become more aware of your own thinking. This will help you make more informed decisions in future practice.

Step 7: Unpacking pedagogical stances

To help you think further about the pedagogical stance that aligns most closely with your own views, we have provided explanations of each stance next so that you can begin to understand them in more detail.

Each example has four sections which address the following:

- Views on learners and learning
- Views on teachers and teaching
- Views on knowledge
- Views on the role (and goals) of schooling

We then also use a building block metaphor to explain how these dimensions work together.

As you read the different accounts of each stance, reflect on the extent to which your chosen stance (from Step 6) aligns with the following corresponding descriptions.

- Which aspects of these descriptions seem most familiar to you?
- Are there any that feel uncomfortable? (If so, why?)

A Traditional view on pedagogy (Niq)

Teachers with Traditional views on pedagogy, such as Niq, see knowledge as an explicit representation of how the world actually is – knowledge is made up of facts. Words, and other symbols such as numbers, carry meaning, which is stable across contexts and learners. Knowledge, what one knows, is a property of an individual.

Traditional teachers see the goal of schooling as being to imbue learners with habits, rules, procedures, and knowledge that have been predefined as being important for the functioning of society.

Teachers with Traditional views on pedagogy see learning as receiving information that the learner can then recall when needed. Learners are seen to have innate abilities which determine their potential to learn. Learners are seen as empty vessels to be filled with knowledge and are not motivated to learn unless provided with extrinsic rewards. Traditional views on pedagogy see learning as an individual activity that involves imitation or acquisition, with teachers seen as experts who hold knowledge.

Teachers with Traditional views on pedagogy believe that breaking information down into small sequential steps is best, they use strategies such as drill and practice, and enhance motivation through the pace of the lesson and introducing competition.

A building block analogy for a traditional pedagogical stance
Traditional teachers see the role of the teacher as to provide building blocks for learners and motivate them to engage with those blocks. A Traditional teacher doesn't concern themselves with what the learner does with those building blocks so long as they can 'show and tell' an appropriate model when necessary.

An individual constructivist view on pedagogy (Sam)

Teachers with an Individual Constructivist view on pedagogy, such as Sam, view knowledge as an explicit representation that an individual has of the world. This representation is a construction and does not represent an objective reality – it is how the world is perceived to be by the individual.

Individual Constructivist teachers see the goal of schooling as being to help young people develop organised, abstract mental models of the world, and procedures for applying them which are transferable across situations.

Learners are seen as being active constructors of their knowledge, and they do this by integrating new information into their existing mental models. However, an Individual Constructivist teacher will believe that a learner's age or stage of development limits the nature of the mental models they can develop – initially being specific representations of particular instances of a phenomenon (concrete representations), which at a later stage will become abstract models that can be applied across contexts. Teachers will therefore believe that younger learners need concrete experiences, whilst older learners can deal with abstract information and refine their mental models through practical problem-solving activities. Individual Constructivist teachers will believe that a learner's mental model doesn't represent an objective external reality but is useful if it fits their experience. They will also believe that learners are intrinsically motivated to make sense of the world and to resolve inconsistencies within their mental models – as such they are self-directed and self-regulated.

Individual Constructivist teachers see the role of the teacher as being to guide learning. Learning is seen as the process of acquisition of new information which then needs to be integrated into the learner's existing mental model – which may mean adapting that mental model so that it better fits with all of the available information. Whilst this process of meaning-making is an individual process, cooperation with others can create cognitive conflicts – by introducing new information that does not align with their existing mental model – which, in turn, leads to learning (re-organising of that mental model to resolve the cognitive conflict).

A building block analogy for individual constructivism

The Individual Constructivist teacher knows that their learners are each constructing their own individual model. The teacher believes their role is to provide the learners with new building blocks that they can incorporate into their individual models. The teacher cannot see the learner's models, and the learners cannot see each other's or the teacher's. Through interaction with individual learners, the teacher tries to imagine what the learner's individual models look like so that they know which building blocks to give them next or how to help them see how to combine their building blocks in new ways to make better models.

A social constructivist view on pedagogy (Aba)

A Social Constructivist teacher, such as Aba, views knowledge as a construction that does not represent an objective reality. Meaning is seen as created through dialogue in communities and knowledge is thus seen as socially constructed.

This teacher sees the goal of schooling as being to help young people develop organised, abstract mental models of the world and procedures for applying them which are transferable across situations. Within this, the teacher sees it as being important that young people understand the nature of subject domains and the ways in which their knowledge bases are socially constructed.

The Social Constructivist teacher sees learners as being active constructors of their knowledge – by integrating new information into their existing mental models. The nature of a learner's mental model is not seen as constrained by their age or stage but by the sophistication of their existing model and the experiences that they have had. Learners are intrinsically motivated to make sense of how others in society see the world. The Social Constructivist teacher believes that this enables the learner to interact meaningfully with other people, and it is through dialogue with others that meaning emerges. The learning process relies on collaboration to co-construct understanding.

The Social Constructivist teacher believes that the role of the teacher is to scaffold learning so that learners develop socially established understanding. The teacher does this by engaging learners in interaction with others – through reconciling their different mental models, learning occurs. Where interaction is with someone (e.g. a peer or teacher) who knows more about the subject than the learner does, they can achieve more than they would be able to achieve on their own - this is known as the 'Zone of Proximal Development' (Vygotsky, 1978).

A building block analogy for social constructivism

The Social Constructivist teacher believes that each individual learner starts out with their own model. When learners collaborate they combine their models so that they end up with one shared model which integrates building blocks from each of their original individual models (and is thus more sophisticated). Each person then takes a copy of that shared model which they retain for future use. The Social Constructivist teacher believes that their role is to direct and scaffold this process.

A sociocultural view on pedagogy (Jo)

A teacher with a Sociocultural view of pedagogy, such as Jo, believes that knowledge is the ability to act in meaningful ways within particular communities, which have shared goals and shared valued ways of working. A Sociocultural teacher believes that knowing and acting are intrinsically linked and that knowledge can be explicit or tacit and emerges through activity.

The Sociocultural teacher sees the goal of schooling as being to support young people in becoming competent in valued social practices, within a range of different communities each of which has its own shared objectives and valued ways of working.

This teacher recognises that learners belong to a range of different communities (i.e. people who have shared purposes and shared valued ways of operating). Learners thus have multiple identities and competencies linked to these communities. Learners are seen as intrinsically motivated to belong to particular communities and be recognised as valued members of them – it is about identity formation (becoming) and participation (belonging). Learners are seen as active and agentive – they participate with others and, through collaboration meanings are mutually agreed on. Learning is thus an appropriation of social understandings within particular communities.

Teachers with Sociocultural beliefs aim to orchestrate support for learners by connecting classroom activities to valued practices in the world. They make meanings explicit for learners to use – recognising that knowledge is the ability to act in valued ways in particular contexts.

A building block analogy for a sociocultural stance

The Sociocultural teacher recognises that there are lots of different things you can do with building blocks and lots of different approaches to building. What is important is that learners understand what model they are trying to build (the purpose) and what the accepted ways of going about building it are. Everyone is seen as being able to make a contribution to a construction, and the teacher's job is to induct them into the appropriate ways of working for the particular model they are creating.

Step 8: Reflecting on theory

This process has taken you through a deeply reflective sequence of steps and then walked you through some complex illustrations of different pedagogical stances. These steps and ideas may have challenged your thinking about pedagogy in ways that you may not have experienced before.

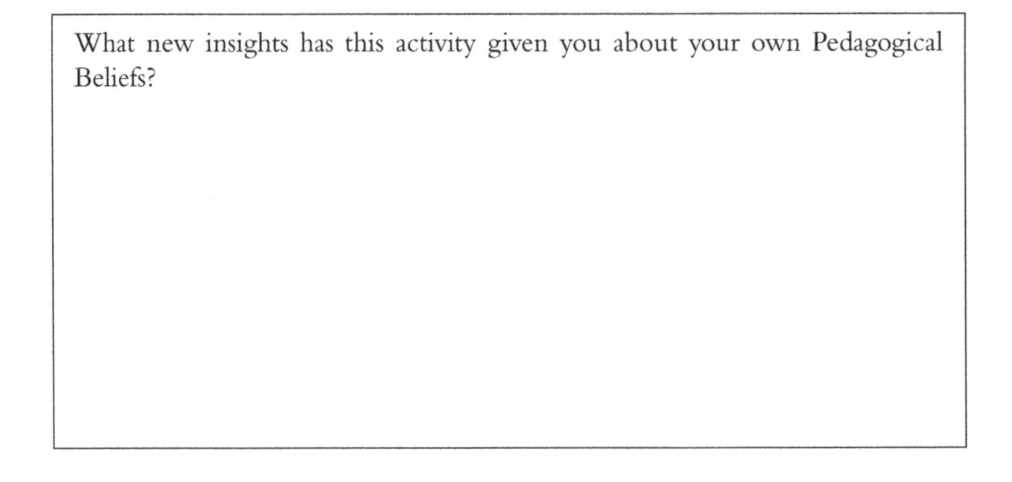
What new insights has this activity given you about your own Pedagogical Beliefs?

Pedagogical beliefs and trends in using digital technology

Earlier in this chapter, we highlighted that there is huge variance across the teaching profession and that you may well have different views to colleagues. In any given school, there is likely to be a wide range of views, values, and beliefs. Let's look at what research evidence tells us about this. For example, TPEA (2022) research found that

> there was a wide range of views on pedagogy, with roughly 25% aligning with a behaviourist [Traditional] view, roughly 60% aligning with a constructivist view, and roughly 15% aligning with a Sociocultural view.

Furthermore, that

> classroom teachers were more likely to align themselves with behaviourist [Traditional] views about pedagogy when talking about knowledge (with leaders more likely to align themselves with Sociocultural views on knowledge), and leaders were more likely to align themselves with behaviourism [Traditional views] when talking about the purpose of schooling (with teachers more likely to align themselves with constructivism).

There is also a body of research which highlights how teacher views on pedagogy change depending on factors such as subject specialism and the age of learners (e.g. Webster et al., 2012).

So why does all this matter?

When thinking about the relationship between our Pedagogical Beliefs and our uses of digital technology, there are two research findings which are useful to draw on.

First, Tondeur et al. (2017) found that teachers with more Traditional Pedagogical Beliefs are less likely to see the use of digital technology in teaching as useful. This aligns with Becker and Riel (1999), who found that teachers with Constructivist beliefs often find it easier to understand the value of using digital technology. There are suggestions from these studies that teachers with particular Pedagogical Beliefs may be more or less likely to utilise digital technology.

However, there is another research finding that is also important to draw on and that relates to a much wider framing of the role of digital technology as one of many tools available to classroom teachers. Hattie and Hamilton (2020) argue that if teachers and leaders are able to choose tools that help them be the teacher or leader that they want to be, then both the tool and the person become more effective. This suggests that if a particular digital technology – as a tool – offers a teacher the means to live out their pedagogical belief, then the digital technology and the teacher become more effective.

In both cases, the teacher's Pedagogical Beliefs are defining decisions about what is used, how it is used, and, most important, why it is being used. With an influence this significant, it is important to understand where those Pedagogical Beliefs come from and how those beliefs are entangled with our wider views about the world around us – including about digital technology. This is what we explore in Chapter 5.

References

Becker, H. J., and Riel, M. M. (1999) 'Teacher Professionalism and the Emergence of Constructivist-Compatible Pedagogies', in *American Educational Research Association*. Montreal: Center for Research on Information Technology and Organizations University of California, Irvine and University of Minnesota, pp. 1–71.

Hamachek, D. (1999) 'Effective Teachers: What They Do, How They Do It, and the Importance of Self-Knowledge', in Lipka, Richard P. and Brinthaupt, Thomas M. (eds) *The Role of Self in Teacher Development*. New York: State University of New York Press.

Hattie, J., and Hamilton, A. (2020) *Why We Focus on the Wrong Drivers in Education*. London: Sage Publications Ltd.

Tondeur, J. et al. (2017) "Understanding the Relationship between Teachers' Pedagogical Beliefs and Technology Use in Education: A Systematic Review of Qualitative Evidence', *Educational Technology Research and Development*, 65(3), pp. 555–575.

TPEA (2022) *Intentions v Reality: What's Really Going on for Our Learners When We Use EdTech?*. Report for Technology, Pedagogy and Education Association.

Twining, P., Browne, N., et al. (2017) *NP3: New Purposes, New Practices, New Pedagogy: Meta-analysis Report*. London: Society for Educational Studies. http://edfutures.net/images/e/e7/NP3_Meta-analysis_report.pdf

Vygotsky, L. (1978) *Mind in Society: Development of Higher Psychological Processes*. Cambridge MA: Harvard University Press.

Webster, A. et al. (2012) *What Influences Teachers to Change Their Practice? a Rapid Research Review*. Bristol: Centre for Understanding Behaviour Change.

CHAPTER

5

What influences pedagogical beliefs and practices?

In the last few chapters, we have introduced four different pedagogical stances (Traditional, Individual Constructivist, Social Constructivist, Sociocultural) and guided you through a process of identifying which you most closely align with.

However, Hamachek (1999, p. 209) is famously quoted as saying,

> Consciously we teach what we know. Unconsciously we teach who we are.

It is helpful to reflect on this when identifying which pedagogical stance we feel aligns with our own values and beliefs. This is because it is entirely possible that we can consciously enact one pedagogical approach whilst unconsciously having beliefs that align with another pedagogical stance. Chapter 6 explores the differences between what we intend to do, what we actually do, and what we believe in more detail. However, to understand why these can vary, it is first important to recognise where our Pedagogical Beliefs come from and what has influenced their formation.

This chapter introduces you to the 'Funnels of Influence' model to help you to identify the influences that are shaping your Pedagogical Beliefs and Practices. The model also provides you with a tool that you can use with colleagues as part of your shared professional learning conversations.

The Funnels of Influence model provides a visual structure that helps to explain the many influences which shape our beliefs and actions. It was originally designed as a tool to aid research about teachers' classroom practices when using digital technology (Aubrey-Smith, 2021).

Like most academic research, the Funnels of Influence model evolved from established research, in this case from Twining et al.'s (2017) Sociocultural framework, which provided a means for unpacking the contextual influences affecting enacted digital practices. Twining et al.'s (2017) framework, in turn, evolved from established Sociocultural theory – drawing on the work of Lave and Wenger (1991). It is important to be aware of how these kinds of models come into existence for

DOI: 10.4324/9781003321637-5

two reasons. First, an understanding of the theoretical basis on which a model is constructed will give you a sense of the quality and quantity of critical literature underpinning the principles of the model itself. Second, each of the iterations and evolutions of any set of theories, literature synthesis, or model developments will have emerged for a specific purpose, in this case in order for digital practices to be meaningfully understood in the context of the many influences affecting them. The purpose of the model itself is important because it has been designed for exactly the purpose that we are now using it for here – to surface and consider the many influences affecting how we choose to use (or not use) digital technology in our teaching and learning provision.

As we begin this explanation, it is important to keep in mind that the Funnels of Influence are always specific to an individual person in a specific place at a specific moment in time. That 'Moment of Practice' may be as short as a few seconds long – because what happens in one moment may affect what happens in the next moment. In academic research, we refer to this kind of conceptualisation as something being 'bounded' – much like a book is bound by its covers – it contains ideas, pages, pictures, and words but has a clear set of boundaries around it at any given time.

A visual representation of the Funnels of Influence can be seen in Figure 5.1. The idea behind the funnel metaphor is that a huge range of influences are being poured downwards towards a given moment in time – continually moving, mixing, and evolving in different ways. The model separates out the many different influences that shape our actions into two overarching groups: first, the Context Funnel (seen on the right of the diagram) and, second, the Self Funnel (seen on the left of the diagram). Influences pour through these funnels, with each layer refining the nature of that influence, and eventually pour out into a third, central funnel – the Situational Funnel. In the Situational Funnel, the combination of influences creates a unique Moment of Practice, which flows out of the bottom of that funnel in the form of Espoused (what we said), Intended (what we planned to do), or Enacted (what we did) Practice.

It's important to keep in mind that the Funnels of Influence represent practice as constantly evolving. Every experience that we have (from a thought or a conversation to a lesson or a course) will affect how we think about other experiences – so the sets of influences are constantly evolving and changing.

Let's now look in greater depth at the key research underpinning the Funnels of Influence model and what each part of the model means in practice. We start with the Context Funnel. This funnel represents all the influences that are *external* to us. Later, we will introduce the Self Funnel which represents all the influences that come from *within* us.

> For a full literature review underpinning the Funnels of Influence, please see Aubrey-Smith, F., (2021) An exploration of the relationship between teachers' pedagogical stance and their use of ICT in classroom practice. Doctoral thesis. The Open University.

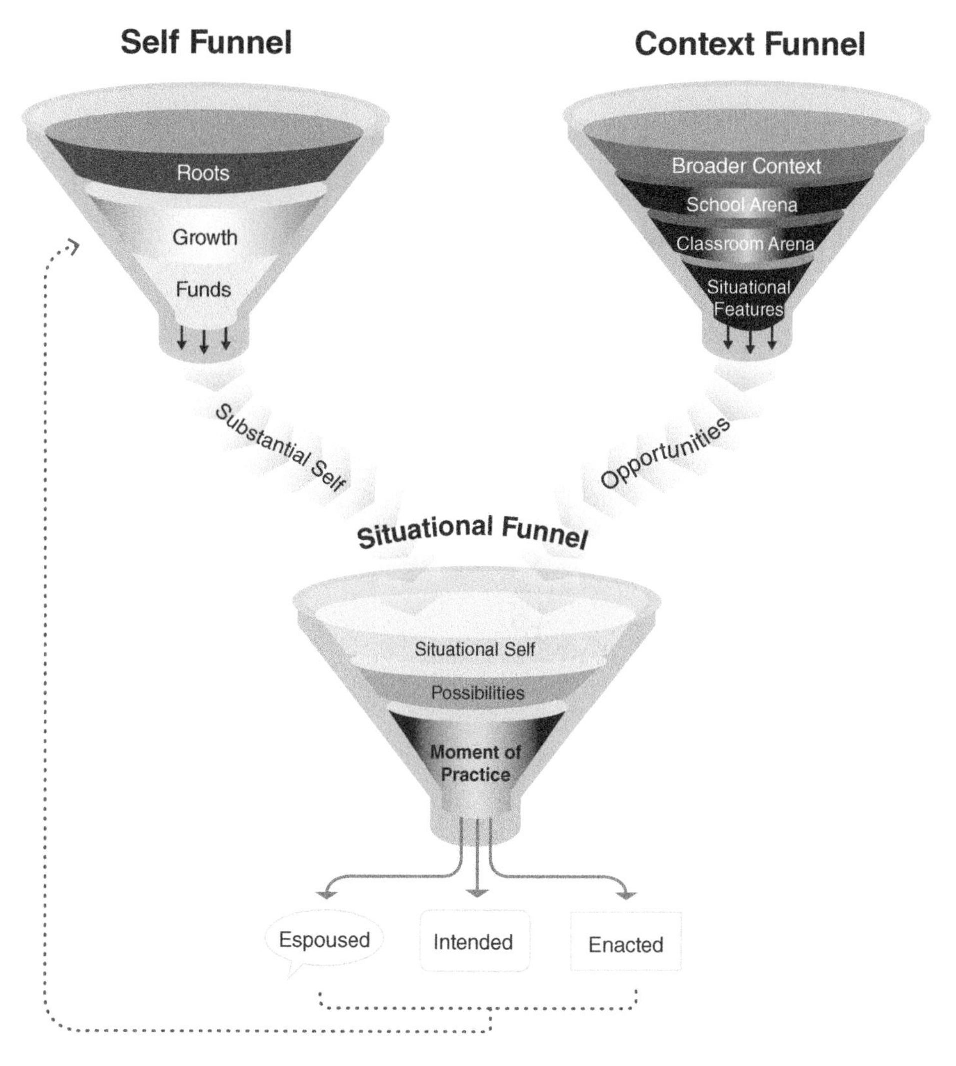

Figure 5.1 The funnels of influence

The context funnel

If you imagine yourself as a teacher within a particular learning scenario, you can start to recognise that there are a great many influences affecting you in that given moment which are external to you. These are conceptualised as flowing through the Context Funnel (seen in Figure 5.2).

There are four layers of influence in this funnel's downward flow: the Broader Context, the School Arena, the Classroom Arena, and Situational Features. The influences are filtered down through the funnel, resulting in Opportunities that are presented to us (seen in Figure 5.2 as the 'output' of the funnel). Let's look at each of these in turn.

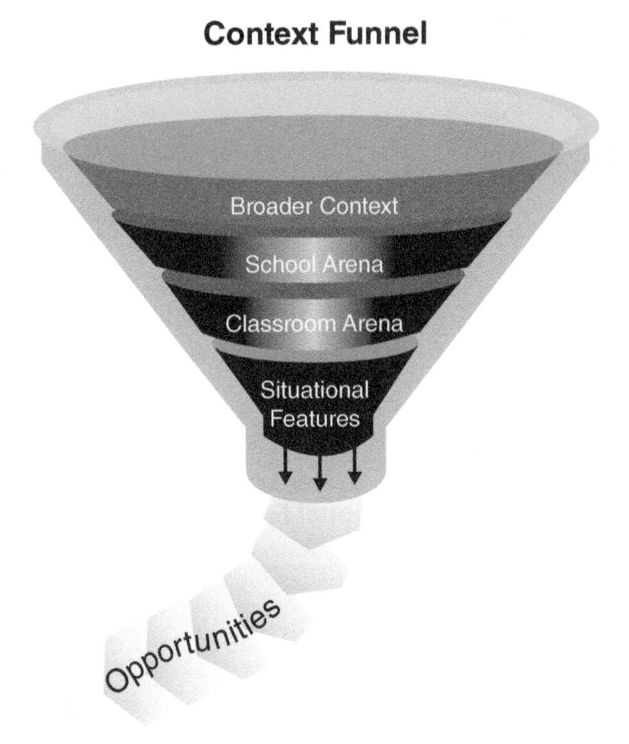

Figure 5.2 The context funnel

Broader context

The top layer of influence is what we have termed the 'Broader Context'. This draws on research by Lave and Wenger (1991) and Garfinkel (1967) as part of their attempts to understand why people do the things that they do in particular contexts. The influences that we are referring to as the Broader Context include cultural, political, global, and national systems and the permeating values and beliefs that these create and embed into communities. These overarching influences shape the landscape we live within and often subliminally influence our thinking, beliefs, and consequent behaviours. These influences affect embedded ideas, such as how our society views childhood and children or where the national tax income is spent. There are many different aspects to this layer of influence – including such things as decisions made by the government and politicians; behaviours of the media; laws that affect how communities behave; economic dynamics; industrial trends; national cultural values and beliefs about the nature of childhood/learners, family, work, education; the nature of social interaction; global disruption by digital technology; and so on. These are the kinds of things that easily highlight the differences between contexts located in central metropolitan London, an Australian Outback town, and a remote village in China.

When talking with teachers and school leaders about influences that are external to a school, there can be a tendency to focus on the limitations of national policy and budgets. These are significant influences. However, it is important that we also think much more broadly – looking at local, regional, other national, and global events, voices, and trends. These are rarely from one person or organisation but, importantly, will shape the way that we interpret the moment that we are in – even if we don't explicitly realise that.

Let's think next about how those Broader Context influences are interpreted by looking at the next layer of influence within this funnel – the School Arena.

School arena

Most of the influences within the Broader Context extend far beyond our professional lives. For example, cultural influences about how a particular society views childhood and children will affect what happens in schools, but it will also affect dynamics within our local area (e.g. decisions about facilities, road safety), economics (e.g. target markets, flexible employment), and laws (e.g. maternity/paternity leave). For the purposes of this book, we are just examining how these Broader Context influences affect classroom practice. Therefore, we are going to apply a kind of filter to those Broader Contextual influences – refining our lens, first, down to the school and, then, down to the classroom.

(Eager readers may recognise that these things affect other things outside of school which indirectly impact how we think about classroom practice. We address that shortly.)

The theorist Jean Lave (1988) encouraged us to think about a concept called an Arena – a space where actors (people), scripts (objects), and plots (routines) combine to set the scene for a particular story to be told (in our case, a Moment of Practice). Within the Funnels of Influence, *School Arena* refers to enduring human and physical features of the school that we work within. These are things that have been interpreted or created as a result of influences from the Broader Context, for example school policies, values, beliefs, facilities, routines, expectations, and staffing – things that remain relatively stable over time and influence our thinking, decisions, and actions. These kinds of influences often emerge from local culture – both explicitly (e.g. behaviour policy reflecting the nature of the school's catchment) and implicitly (e.g. perceived parental expectations). Furthermore, some of these influences are usually very stable (e.g. the features of a school building or the socioeconomic intake of the staff and student body), and some of the features are more changeable (e.g. where individual staff are deployed in a given year or a strategic school improvement priority).

Good examples of School Arena influences might be the following:

- facilities available at the school (e.g. a library, classrooms, a school hall)
- norms (e.g. a ringing bell to indicate the end of a lesson)

- expectations (e.g. that learners are in classes of 30 – grouped by age and overseen by one teacher who is addressed as Miss or Sir)

Classroom arena

Given that we are thinking specifically about classroom practice, focusing on influences at the school level is rather problematic because it encourages us to be too generalised in our thinking. To help us with this, it is useful to draw on earlier work by Lave (1988), who encouraged us to think about a specific combination of human and physical features within which practice takes place (e.g. a classroom) and which are not routinely changed but which are specific to the space the teacher is in.

The Funnels of Influence therefore refers to the Classroom Arena as a subset of the School Arena. This refers to relatively stable contextual features which are specific to an individual classroom within a school – and which may differ from other classrooms within the same school.

Good examples of Classroom Arena influences might be the following:

- availability of particular classroom furniture (e.g. moveable tables)
- the presence of a fixed digital board or a set of laptops
- a particular teacher and support staff assigned to a specific class

It is important to remember that at this stage, we are still thinking about contextual influences rather than our interpretations of them. A good illustration of this is the concept of 'a class of learners'. Let's imagine that one day, 5 out of 30 learners from your class were ill and absent from school. The 30 learners still represent 'the class' (and thus will inform the teacher's planning and thinking) even if 5 of them are absent. This makes the concept of 'the class' both *stable* (as the teacher is still responsible for them) and *situational* (due to the absence of five learners) at the same time. The stable element is part of the Classroom Arena. The less stable elements form part of the Situational Features.

Situational features

Whilst the Classroom Arena includes all those features of the classroom that are relatively stable, the Situational Features refer to the less stable elements of the context. For example, if you do not usually have a class set of laptops, but for one particular learning activity you did have 1:1 device provision in your classroom, those devices would be Situational Features.

Similarly, by our being in a given context, we change the dynamics of that context – even if we do nothing. For example, by our being in a room, other people will change what they say and do (think of a classroom full of learners and how their behaviour changes as a teacher walks into the room – even before the teacher speaks). Your presence is a Situational Feature.

Some Situational Features are not aspects of the Classroom or School Arena. For example, if there was a lightning storm which caused a power cut so that you could no longer use any of your mains powered digital devices, this would be a Situational Feature. Situational Features are the aspects of the context that may be familiar but that have the potential to change from moment to moment.

Opportunities

The consequence of the influences from the Context Funnel can be thought of as 'Opportunities'. These are sets of circumstances that create the potential for us to engage with something.

Examples of Opportunities might be the following:

- The Opportunity to use 1:1 devices with learners due to the one-off availability of a class set of devices (Situational Feature) combined with a school expectation that digital technology will be used to enhance learning (School Arena) plus a growing pressure for young people to become digitally literate (Broader Context)
- The Opportunity to have two groups of learners working with an adult due to the regular presence of a teaching assistant plus the class teacher (Classroom Arena) and the expectation that teaching assistants will work with small groups (School Arena) in a context in which a high adult to learner ratio is perceived as enhancing learning (Broader Context)

However, as Twining et al. (2017) highlighted, there are other influences (discussed shortly) that affect whether we actually see these Opportunities as being available or relevant to us (these are called Possibilities – explained shortly).

The layers of influence from within the Context Funnel and how they create Opportunities are important to recognise. Often, when we talk about the features of our context that influence our practice, we have a tendency to think of them all collectively. Yet, as the earlier descriptions illustrate, each influence provides a specific set of dynamics that not only directly filter down to us but also affect our colleagues, learners, and our broader communities – creating another kind of circular influence through organisational norms, expectations, and localised culture.

> If you are particularly interested in how each of us influences each other, you may wish to read Bourdieu's work relating to Habitus, Field and Capital - see Bourdieu, P. (1986) 'The Forms of Capital', in Richardson, J. (ed.) Handbook of Theory and Research for the Sociology of Education. Connecticut: Greenwood Press, pp. 241–256, and Bronfenbrenner's work relating to Ecological Systems Theory.
>
> - see Bronfenbrenner, U. (2009) *The Ecology of Human Development: Experiments by Nature and Design.* Cambridge, Massachusetts: Harvard University Press

The self funnel

The Self Funnel can be similarly unpacked. As you will see from Figure 5.3, there are three layers to this funnel: Roots, Growth, and Funds. These result in an influence known as the Substantial Self. That Substantial Self influences how we each see and interpret the world around us, including the Opportunities that flow from the Context Funnel. This is why each of us interprets 'the same' context differently.

Let's look at each of these aspects of the Self Funnel in turn.

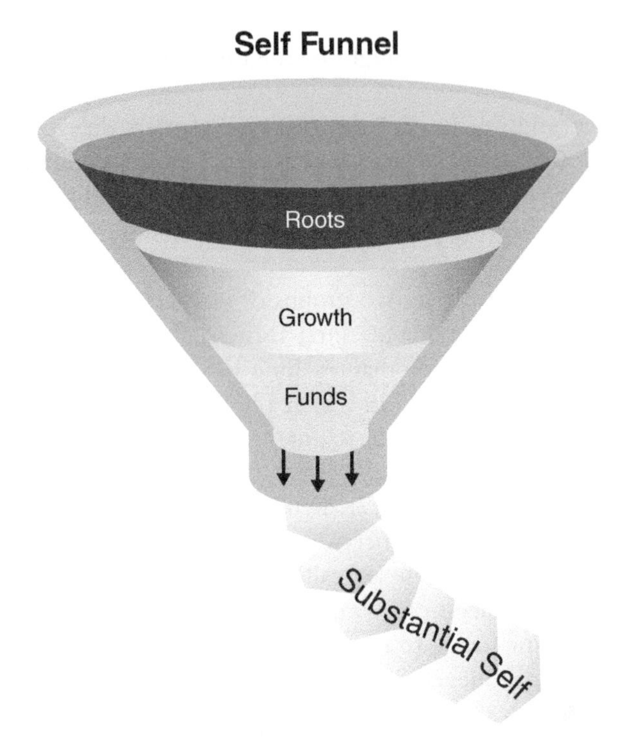

Figure 5.3 The self funnel

Roots

Drawing on the work of Abercrombie (1993) and Nias (1993), the Self Funnel begins with what we describe as Roots. Roots are the influences that shape our formative years from birth – arguably from pre-birth (Grayling, 2011). For example, the social ideologies, norms, values, and belief systems that we are born into, the culture and subcultures that we are raised within, and the associated culturally informed elements of self (such as age, gender, and health). These Roots create a kind of lens that we then see our lives through – including seeding our values.

Those deeply rooted values consequently manifest themselves through other more tangible or conscious beliefs creating a much more subtle influence and a complex network of linked belief sub-systems (Usó-Doménech & Nescolarde-Selva, 2016; Rokeach, 1985). Our Roots are unique to each of us, although we may share aspects with others.

Growth

As we start to live through different experiences, we see, engage with, digest, and reflect on experiences all through the lens of our Roots. These formative experiences build up over time, with each experience shaping and refining the next one as we begin to form ideas about who we are and what our place in the world might be. We refer to this spiral, cumulative process as our Growth. Growth can be thought of as an ever-evolving lens, which combines with Roots to form a composite lens through which we see the world.

In the context of this book, one of the most relevant parts of our Growth relates to how we begin to form ideas about what it means to be a teacher. For example, Beijaard, Meijer, and Verloop (2004) argue that the conceptualisation of a teacher's pedagogical stance begins even before any thoughts about becoming a teacher. Chang-Kredl and Kingsley (2014) argue that teachers interpret Pedagogical Practices through a lens influenced by memories of childhood teachers. Our experiences of our own childhood teachers directly shape what we think the role of a teacher should or should not be – a view which then frames how we see our later or current professional role.

Funds

As we grow, we learn and our knowledge increases. In a teaching context, Moll et al. 1992) talk about this as Funds of Knowledge – a phrase which emerged from the anthropological research of Vélez-Ibáñez and Greenberg (1992). These Funds of Knowledge can be thought of as specific to the different domains that we operate within and which are an embedded part of our Growth – our accumulated experiences. These Funds form part of the composite lens through which a person views and assimilates new information.

Substantial self

Informed by the notion of Funds of Knowledge, Esteban-Guitart and Moll (2014) introduced the idea of Funds of Identity – the gathering of experiences which accumulate and shape our understanding of ourselves. These all shape what Rogers and Scott (2008) call our Substantial Self – the inner version of ourselves that enables us to draw meaning from experiences that we have in our lives.

The Substantial Self might best be thought of as the meaning-maker within ourselves. It is that part of our inner identity which contains our Roots, our

Growth and those Funds of Knowledge and Identity, and forms the Self that is consistent across all kinds of contexts – the values and deeply held beliefs about the world around us. It forms part of the composite lens made up of Roots, Growth, and our Funds of Knowledge.

To understand the significance of our Substantial Self and its implications requires us to have some understanding of the theories around Identity (e.g. Beauchamp and Thomas, 2009; Olsen, 2008). Put simply, our identity is who we imagine ourselves to be in any given moment – affecting our confidence, our vocabulary, our perception of how others might see us, and our decisions about what to wear, what to say, and what to do (see Pillen, Den Brok and Beijaard, 2013; Beauchamp and Thomas, 2009; Korthagen, 2004; Hargreaves, 2000; Beijaard, Verloop and Vermunt, 1999). Our identity is influenced (but not defined) by others as well as by ourselves. Furthermore, identity can be fluid – changing from experience to experience, or even from moment to moment, depending on the Situational influences affecting us. We may hold multiple identities at the same time, and we may or may not be aware that we are doing so.

Yet amongst all these many multiple identities, there will be stable features – usually values-based and deeply rooted. It is that enduring sense of Self – which Korthagen (2004) refers to as inner mission – which we describe here as our Substantial Self. We cannot make this form of Self tangible because we are always present in a context (and thus Situational), but it exists within us and permeates our other identities.

When the funnels of influence combine

Having explored the influences that pour into and through each of the two funnels of influence – the Context Funnel and the Self Funnel – we will now explain how these combine – as illustrated in Figure 5.4.

Opportunities from the Context Funnel are viewed through the lens of our Substantial Self (from the Self Funnel), in a particular Moment in time, creating a Situation. That Situation will have characteristics that are absolutely unique to that particular combination of influences at that specific moment in time. A Situation can never be fully replicated because of its time-bounded nature.

Within that Situation, there are many influences that affect what then happens. However, these are all *a direct result* of the way in which we view the contextual Opportunities through the lens of the Substantial Self.

First, we form a Situational Identity – our Situational Self. This is not usually a conscious formation but a response to a situation that we find ourselves in and what we bring to it from within us. That very specific Situational Identity affects our consequent thinking – what we say, what we intend to do, and what we enact in practice. But we may or may not be aware of these subtleties. A Situational Self is not a persona that we adopt; it is a subconscious set of characteristics that can be incredibly subtle and often implicit. These different elements

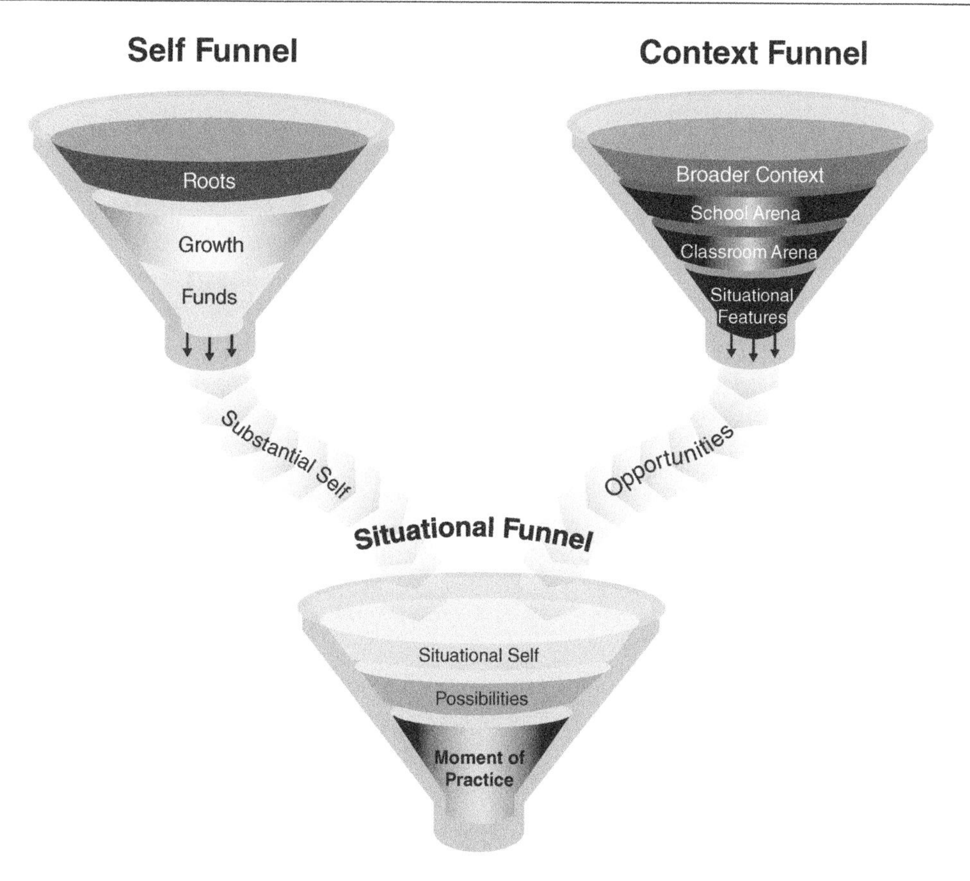

Figure 5.4 The situational funnel

will vary depending on where we are, who we are with, what our aspirations are, and a whole range of other influences. For example, our Situational Identity as a teacher when it's just us and our class might be subtly different to our Situational Identity when presenting in front of the senior leadership team. Our Situational Identity with one class of learners might feel different to our Situational identity when with another class of learners. It is the context that is affecting how we see ourselves.

The subconscious nature of our Situational Self is important to note because how we see ourselves in that given moment will define what we believe we can take up from the Opportunities flowing from the Context Funnel – what we perceive to be possible in that Moment.

Thus, our Situational Self interacts with the Opportunities offered by the context to create Possibilities for us in that moment. For example, if a trolley of laptops is present in our classroom that is an Opportunity – it is physically there and available for us to use. But once we know it is there, it may also become a Possibility – if we can see how we could use it with that particular group of learners, given factors such as their needs, our level of technical competence, and our understanding of

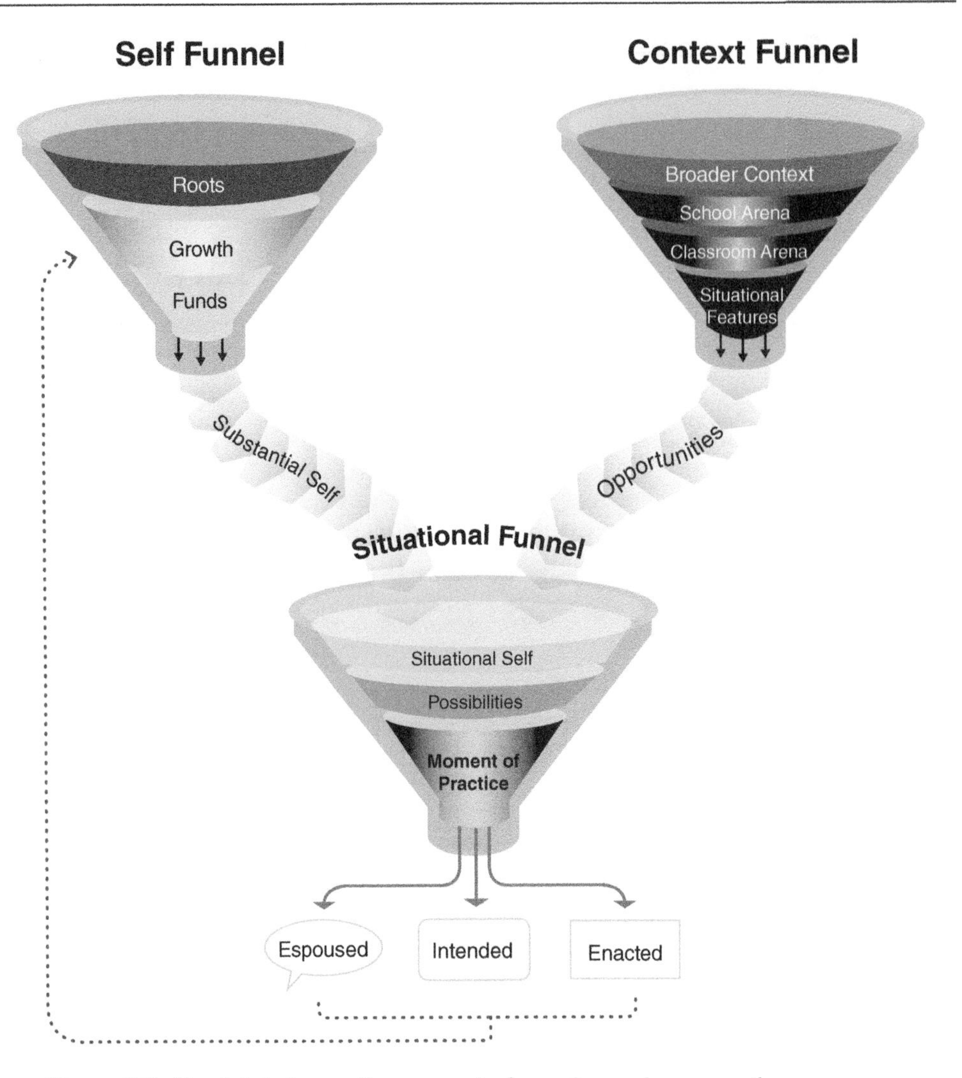

Figure 5.5 The link between the moment of practice and our growth

how it would enhance their learning. Those perceptions will be specific to our Situational Self.

Our Situational Self is specific to a unique Moment in time, and it is important to remember that a Moment may only be a matter of seconds. Every action, experience, or interaction involving us or taking place around us perpetually shapes how we perceive the next Moment. This relationship can be seen in Figure 5.5 through the arrow going from the Moment of Practice back towards Growth.

For example, right now, as you read this page, the ideas that we are discussing will create, refine, disrupt, confirm, or challenge aspects of your existing knowledge. This will immediately affect how you interpret and respond to what happens next. Our Growth is thus dynamic: constantly evolving and adapting to every future moment based on each prior moment.

All of these influences combine to shape what we implicitly believe – as seen through the following:

- what we say (Espoused Beliefs)
- what we plan to do (Intended Practice)
- what we do in practice (Enacted Practice)

Hopefully, you are starting to become more aware of the many influences that can make subtle or profound differences to your decisions, your language, your reflections, your perceptions, and so much more.

The reason that this is so important to explore is because understanding these influences helps us think about how we come to form our Pedagogical Beliefs and about the influences that have an impact on us. It helps us recognise what we could change about ourselves and our own practices. Having greater precision in understanding our beliefs and practice enables us to more accurately fine-tune future practice to ensure alignment between what we believe, what we intend to do, and what we enact.

We have taken you through some complex theory that draws on ideas from education, sociology, psychology, cognitive neurology, philosophy, and anthropology. The Funnels of Influence model brings these ideas together in order to provide a structured way of thinking about the influences that affect our practice when using digital technology to support learning. We are now going to walk you through a guided activity which will help you unpack these ideas in a way that is meaningful to you personally.

Guided Activity 5.1: Understanding your own funnels of influence

Purpose: To help you to become more aware of the influences affecting your practice.

It is important that you take time to think deeply, critically, and reflectively about each step that we take you through.

Time Required: 1 hour

- Step 1: Identifying your chosen Moment of Practice
- Step 2: Unpacking your Context
- Step 3: Unpacking your Self
- Step 4: Unpacking your Situation
- Step 5: Reflection

How to use this guided activity

To make sense of the earlier theoretical explanation, it is helpful to unpack an example that you are very familiar with – your own practice. This guided activity has five steps to it which are all centred on a specific and recent activity that you have carried out with your class. In relation to that activity, we will first unpack the Context Funnel. Then we will unpack the Self Funnel (you), and then we will unpack the Situational Funnel.

However, there are many additional ways that you can use this activity, for example to support colleagues in unpacking the influences on their practices, identify the influences affecting specific colleagues in order to more effectively support them with their uses of digital technology, or analyse influences affecting particular learners as part of your own reflective practice or practitioner research.

There are three key factors to bear in mind whilst you are utilising the Funnels of Influence. The first is that it is a model that exists to unpack specific Moments of Practice in relation to the individual person enacting them. You cannot use this model to analyse group behaviours because each individual person will bring their own influences from the Self Funnel which will affect the Situational Funnel and thus the output. You could, however, invite each person within a group to unpack a shared event or activity in order to reveal the different perspectives and lived experiences of it. But the emphasis must remain on each individual person. Be cautious not to be tempted to look for 'common themes' because this will shift the focus unduly towards the Context and away from the Self.

The second point is that if we unpack the many different influences that affect what we think, say, intend, and do honestly and openly, we will discover that we are making many decisions without necessarily being aware that we are doing so. Sometimes these are habits or routines, sometimes these are subconsciously adopted behaviours, and sometimes these are instinctive responses. By unpacking the layers of influences, we are making these influences more visible. This encourages us to be more reflective – considering if we wish to continue our historic decisions or whether we wish to refine, adapt, or reconsider our approach to future decisions.

The final point cautions against focusing too much on the Context. This is important because evidence shows that as a teaching profession, we often focus disproportionately on externalised issues and influences rather than recognising our role within them (Durrant, 2019; Priestley et al., 2015) – in other words, the influences coming from the Self Funnel. As teachers, we often have more agency than we think. In other words, there are more opportunities for us to make meaningful decisions about our own practice than we necessarily currently realise. It is likely that you will see this illustrated as you work through this Guided Activity.

We strongly recommend you use the editable version of this Guided Activity, which you can download from www.onelifelearning.co.uk/resources

Step 1: Identifying your chosen moment of practice

Identify a specific activity within your recent teaching practice in which digital technology was involved (e.g. an activity that your learners completed). For the purposes of this step, we are going to first look at that activity as a whole and then later draw out a specific Moment of Practice within it.

Your first action is to surface detail about your chosen activity. You will need this detail in order to be able to meaningfully unpack the range of influences affecting your practice.

Each row in the tables that follow surfaces a different aspect of the Moment of Practice. In the left column, there are overarching questions, and then a series of sub-questions which should help you to probe deeply into the Moment of Practice that you are analysing. In the right column, there is an example response to illustrate the kinds of ideas that you may wish to record. These sample responses are taken from a case study which unpacked the ways in which digital technology was used by a teacher with Social Constructivist beliefs (Aubrey-Smith, 2021, p.108).

(a) Which day did this activity take place on? What else was happening that day? Were there any significant events before/after?	*(e.g. Tuesday morning maths lesson with Year 6 – 4 weeks before national assessments.)*
(b) What time of day did this activity take place? How did that affect the mindset of those involved? (e.g. hunger, tiredness)	*(e.g. 10 a.m. lesson – just after short morning break.)*

(c) Where (exactly) did this activity take place? Was there anything unusual about the location or surroundings at the time?	*(e.g. Usual classroom, windy day – learners full of energy.)*
(d) Which learners were part of this activity? How were they chosen or identified, and by whom?	*(e.g. Whole class present, teacher working with target individuals located in pairs around the classroom amongst other peers.)*
(e) Who was in the same room (or specific place)? If there were learners not involved in this activity, what were they doing? What were other adults doing?	*(e.g. The teacher was working with a group of learners who needed specific interventions – with skills gaps identified by a recent practice test paper.)*
(f) What were the intended outcomes of the activity? Who defined the activity-specific outcomes?	*(e.g. For targeted learners to identify specific mathematical knowledge gaps and work with a peer or teacher to close those gaps.)*

(g) What was the content of the activity?	*(e.g. Learners listed the concepts they were not secure on in their practice maths test paper. They then prioritised one to focus on first. Learners accessed specific pre-recorded 'how to' videos made by the teacher – accessed via the school YouTube channel. They watched, rewatched, paused, and practised the relevant skill, discussing issues with a peer or the teacher as necessary.)*
(h) Who chose the content? Who created the activity? The lesson plan? The short-, medium-, and longer-term plans that this was part of?	*(e.g. The school decided to have a school YouTube channel for teachers to store pre-recorded 'how to' videos. Individual teachers decide when and how to record and utilise those videos in classrooms. This lesson was part of a year-group planned revision block in preparation for national tests. Individual teachers in the year group decided what learners in their class needed to revise, how, and why.)*

(i) What proportion (roughly) of the time during this activity: - Was the teacher talking? - Were learners working independently? - Were learners working with each other?	*(e.g. The teacher introduced the process for revising this lesson at the start. Learners then worked independently to begin with. However, the teacher intentionally sat learners together who were going to be revising the same topic and encouraged them to talk to each other about what they were doing, how they were doing it, and how they were overcoming difficulties. The teacher watched, listened, and then joined the conversations when their intervention prevented misconceptions or consolidated learning.)*
(j) Any other relevant information about this activity	*(e.g. Learners in this class were used to accessing pre-recorded teacher videos on demand and being able to rewatch them before, during, or after lessons. This was a part of usual practice across the school.)*

Now, let's think in more detail about a specific Moment of Practice within that activity (e.g. a specific interaction that you had with a learner, a section of the activity during which you were providing some form of input, or a moment when you were aware of an issue that arose even if you decided not to intervene).

(k) How would you summarise that Moment of Practice? Include: when and where the moment took place, who was involved and what they did/ said, what resources were involved and how they were being used and why you did what you did.	*(e.g. The specific Moment was one in which two girls were struggling with the same process – multiplying two 2-digit numbers. The girls had watched the 'how to' video and were trying to apply the process using paper and pencil but forgetting a key step and getting stuck. The teacher observed them struggling and gently asked them to verbalise their process. The teacher asked the learners to re-watch the 'how to' video and write themselves instructions as they watched it – then use those instructions to complete a practice example. The girls did this and discovered for themselves the key step they had previously been forgetting. The teacher explained that they wanted the learners to discover the error for themselves rather than be explicitly told so that they understood the whole process and were more likely to remember it.)*
(l) Who took the lead in this particular Moment of Practice? Was this instigated by you as a teacher, a learner, or another adult? Why was that the case?	*(e.g. The teacher intervened at a vital point in the task when they saw a misconception arise. The practice was otherwise taking place independently of the teacher [although defined by the teacher].)*

(m) What were the Outcomes of that Moment of Practice?	*(e.g. The girls were able to complete the practice problem that they had been stuck on, as well as additional examples, and were later able to articulate how to go about the problem in future. They also spoke about how they liked the strategy of writing their own instructions based on a 'how to' video – and how they would use that approach in other lessons and contexts.)*

Step 2: Unpacking your context

We are now going to unpack the Context Funnel by inviting you to consider each layer in reverse (Situational Features, Classroom Arena, School Arena, Broader Context). It is easier to unpack the Context Funnel in reverse order because we then start with the features which are most familiar and then gradually move away from that familiarity.

(a) Situational Features Describe any features of the context that were specific to that moment of practice	*(e.g. Whole-class lesson with the teacher working with targeted pairs of learners for the purposes of intervention – focused on content revision in order to raise test outcomes.)*

(b) Classroom Arena Describe the stable features of your classroom (e.g. the layout, what furniture and equipment you had and how they were organised, how many children in the class and their characteristics	*(e.g. The classroom had tables in different permutations – some clusters, some individual tables, some rows. There was no 'front' to the classroom – the teacher moved fluidly around the room based on conversation and need. There was a trolley of laptops for learners to access on demand, and these were used as and when learners wanted them – with children passing them around to peers when they needed/finished with them. The classroom contained 32 children including those with Special Educational Needs or Disabilities [SEND] supported in the mainstream. There was one teacher and no other adults present.).*
(c) School Arena Describe the School Arena. (e.g. relevant policy expectations and school norms, school ethos, how the school day was organised, what facilities and resources were available, which staff were involved and why)	*(e.g. This mainstream co-ed state school was populated by learners from low to mid social economic backgrounds, with an average % of those with special educational needs. The school followed national norms in terms of policy, curriculum, timetabling and staffing. The school ethos was to promote independent learning. The school budget was pressurised, and so there were no additional support staff available in class – the use of pre-recorded teacher films was introduced in part to provide teacher capacity by reducing the need for teachers to repeat process instructions multiple times within the same lesson.)*

(d) Broader Context Describe key elements of the Broader Context (e.g. the role of the media, relevant laws, economic pressures, political issues, views on children and childhood, views on digital technology)	*(e.g. The role of the school YouTube channel had been influenced by a national network encouraging Flipped Learning approaches. The political environment emphasised the importance of test outcomes.)*
(e) Opportunities What Opportunities were available in that Moment of Practice as a result of the influences coming from the Context (Broader Context, School Arena, Classroom Arena, and Situational Features – as outlined in parts a–d of this table)?	*(e.g. Teacher has time to work with pairs of learners because the other learners are being supported by the video clips on the YouTube channel and were used to working in this way.)*

Step 3: Unpacking your self

We are now going to unpack the Self Funnel by inviting you to consider each layer in order (Roots, Growth, Funds). When unpacking the Self Funnel, it is easier to do this in chronological order because our memories tend to remember the most significant events – thereby acting as a handy filter.

Roots	
(a) How would you describe the life that you were born into and the values that it introduced you to? (e.g. home environment, significant people, culture, religion, social and economic norms, values and beliefs about gender, age, dis/ability, etc.)	*(e.g. The teacher spoke about their Traditional English upper-working-class home environment, the full-time employed roles of their parents, and their sense of comparison to their siblings – in a home environment and national culture where social comparison and academic achievements were fore-fronted.)*
Growth	
(b) Who were your significant childhood teachers and why were they significant?	*(e.g. The teacher's significant childhood teachers were those who had provided personalised guidance and support, and gentle encouragement – investing time 1:1 to help overcome specific issues.)*

(c) Why did you decide to become a teacher?	*(e.g. This teacher became a teacher in order to help others to overcome specific difficulties.)*
(d) What was your route into teaching, and how did that shape you as a teacher?	*(e.g. This teacher took a school-based route into teaching – completing more classroom practice experience before and during training than was formally required – specifically to mitigate a low level of self-confidence.)*
(e) What have been the most formative experiences that you have had as a teacher, and why did they make an impact on you?	*(e.g. This teacher benefitted from gentle coaching by colleagues and leaders – which they felt brought out their skills. This was seen to be a continuation of valuing the personal and a targeted approach to helping others to learn.)*

(f) Where have your beliefs about what good teaching and learning look like evolved from?	*(e.g. This teacher explicitly wanted to replicate the supportive practice they had experienced themselves as a child – namely care, individual time and attention and helping learners overcome personal challenges.)*
(g) How would you describe your previous experiences with digital technology at school/in your professional roles? - Digital skills - Confidence - Self-expectations - Expectations from others	*(e.g. This teacher described themself as an 'average' user – using the technology that was available but looking out for different ways that it could be used to support individual learner needs.)*
(h) How would you describe your experiences with digital technology in relation to your life beyond school? - Home/domestic tasks - Social interaction - Lifestyle uses (e.g. hobbies and well-being) - Personal learning - Creativity (e.g. making things)	*(e.g. This teacher did not particularly use a lot of technology beyond school – functional apps and devices to support their specific tasks and needs in everyday life.)*

(i) How do other people in your life influence your relationship with digital technology?	*(e.g. This teacher spoke about family members who they perceived as more confident when using digital technology. They also spoke about specific colleagues who they perceived as more competent. The teacher saw this as happening in parallel to their own experiences – with family/colleagues using digital technology for other kinds of purposes).*
(j) Describe any other experiences you have had in your life that seem relevant	*(e.g. The teacher liked working in an environment which supported professional risk-taking – they saw this as providing a safety net to try out new ideas, which in turn boosted their confidence to experiment with different pedagogical approaches)*
Funds	
(k) In that Moment of Practice, how would you describe your **Identity**? (e.g. how confident and capable did you feel as a teacher?)	*(e.g. The teacher felt that they were nurturing the individual learners – identifying their specific needs, and sensitively coaching them through overcoming task-specific issues, in parallel to teaching them strategies that they could apply to similar problems in future.)*

(l) In that Moment of Practice, how would you describe your **Knowledge** (e.g. about the topic you were teaching, prior experiences of the topic and/ or with the learners, and/or with the digital technology)	*(e.g. The teacher recognised that they were able to intervene appropriately due to their subject knowledge, pedagogical knowledge, subject knowledge, and knowledge of their learners' behaviours and characteristics.)*
(m) What knowledge were you utilising in your **role** as the Teacher? (e.g. were you gaining knowledge - *with* the learners, - *from* the learners or - providing the knowledge to the learners?)	*(e.g. This teacher was providing a solution for the learners which the learners then adopted.)*
Substantial Self	
(n) Which aspects of your Self do you feel are stable or consistent across contexts?	*(e.g. This teacher's Substantial Self emerges through the role of supporting others and the impact made on others both the short and longer term.)*

Step 4: Unpacking your situation

Next let's have a think about how the Context Funnel and the Self Funnel combine. Importantly, these are located 'in the Moment of Practice'

Situational Self What identity do you feel that you have in this specific Situation at a particular 'Moment of Practice'? How does this Situational Identity relate to the other people who are also in that Moment? How does it affect your actions? Which influences (from the Self and/or the Context) particularly shaped this identity, and why?	*(e.g. When responding to the individual learner, the teacher saw their relationship with them as having the potential to impact their lives in both the short and long term. The teacher trusted the learners – having deliberately built purposeful and positive relationships with their class.* *These ideas stemmed from their own childhood perception of effective teacher intervention and relationships and were supported by a context that encouraged risk-taking and innovative approaches to supporting learning.)*
Possibilities Which of these Opportunities did you *feel* were available to you 'in the Moment of Practice', based on your *perception* of the Situation? Which influences (from the Self and/or the Context), particularly shaped your interpretation of the Opportunities available to you, and why?	*(e.g. In the Moment of Practice, the teacher felt confident in their ability to manage the class and support their learning. This was because they had created and uploaded screen recordings and films to support learners in the past and found it very effective – encouraging learner autonomy and creating teacher capacity to provide intervention.)*

Step 5: Reflection

Steps 1–4 invited you to identify a Moment of Practice – a particular activity that you carried out with your learners. You were asked to unpack some key details about that activity, then to unpack a number of influences from the Context Funnel and a number of influences from the Self Funnel, and finally to consider the Situational Funnel.

This process is most effectively carried out as a coached discussion. It works best when you write down or tell someone about your initial reactions, and they then encourage you to dig deeper, asking, 'Why do you think that?' 'What other interpretations could there be?' or 'How do you know?'

In this book format, we invite you now to seek to replicate that process by challenging yourself to go back through your earlier notes and consider for each point 'What makes me think that way?' 'What else might be influencing me?' and 'What am I not seeing but is influencing this?' Importantly, ask, 'How do I *know*?' – ensuring that you are drawing on evidence and not speculation or assumptions.

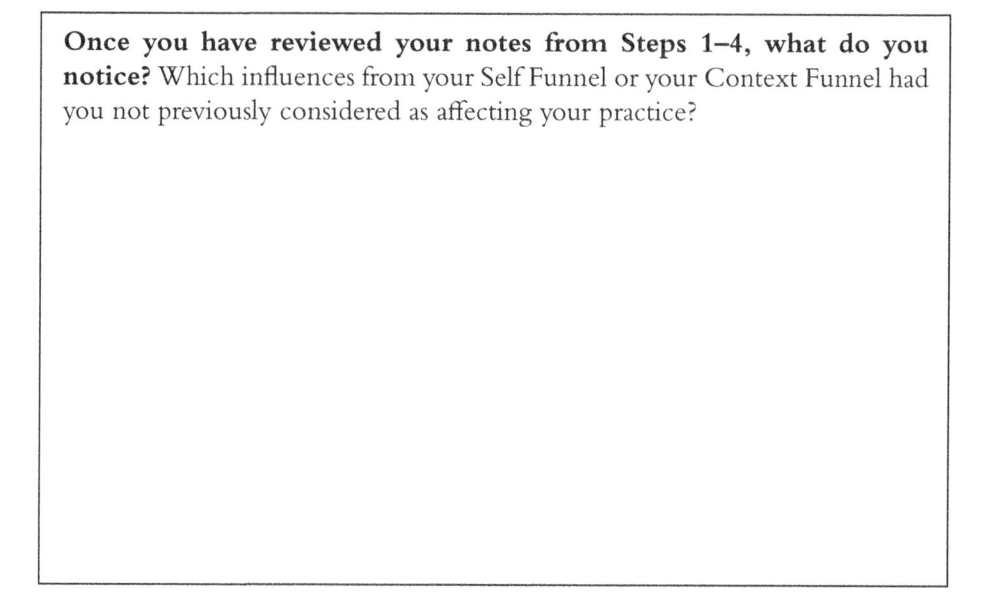

Once you have reviewed your notes from Steps 1–4, what do you notice? Which influences from your Self Funnel or your Context Funnel had you not previously considered as affecting your practice?

Sometimes, when people do this task for the first time, they rush through it and only capture surface-level detail. This makes the reflection process ineffective. If you find that you are reviewing your notes but not seeing any patterns, insights, or surprises emerge, it probably means that you are not surfacing enough detail. You will benefit from working through Steps 1–4 again and really challenging yourself to think about where your 'blind spots' may be. You may find it helpful to invite a colleague to engage in conversation with you about this – by explaining our ideas aloud we often surface aspects that we might not surface when working in isolation.

Another way to help draw insights out is to reflect on two aspects from that Moment of Practice – one significant strength and one point of friction.

SIGNIFICANT STRENGTH

Identify one very specific detail about your chosen Moment of Practice that you feel particularly **proud** about (e.g. a phrase, a tone of voice, a response, an idea).

Write it here:

Now reread your notes from Guided Activity 5.1 Steps 2 and 3. Where did that Strength emerge from? See if you can identify an influence from each of the layers in each of the Funnels that led to that strength.

POINT OF FRICTION

Identify one very specific detail about your chosen Moment of Practice that you feel was a point of **friction** for you personally (e.g. a decision that you did not want to make, a question that arose in your mind, a challenging interaction with a learner that you did not know how to handle).

Write a summary of it here:

Now reread your notes from Guided Activity 5.1 Steps 2–4 again. Why did that Point of Friction arise? See if you can identify an influence from each of the layers in each of the Funnels that led to that point of friction.

Conclusion

This activity is a challenging one to undertake on your own, and you may benefit from working through it with a supportive colleague who has some coaching experience. However, we hope that the process of identifying, unpacking, and reflecting on the influences on your practice is starting to help you think more precisely.

For any Moment of Practice, it is a powerful point of reflection to identify the influences that are shaping it. By doing so, we become able to identify where we then have agency to do the following:

- make different kinds of decisions in our future practice or
- reconsider our beliefs

In this chapter, we have introduced you to the Funnels of Influence model and given you a very brief introduction to some of the theory that explains why we each think and do the things that we think and do.

The reason that we have introduced this to you as part of this book is to help you uncover and reflect on the many influences that shape the decisions that you make about using digital technology to support learning. Much of what we believe is tacit – we are not aware of it – and yet it still influences what we think and do. By surfacing our beliefs, we develop a greater understanding of the decisions we are making. In turn, this helps us seek greater alignment between our beliefs and our actions (moving from pedagogy to effective pedagogy).

References

Abercrombie, M. L. J. (1993) *The Anatomy of Judgement: An Investigation into the Processes of Perception and Reason*. Harmondsworth: Penguin.

Aubrey-Smith, F. (2021) *An exploration of the relationship between teachers' pedagogical stance and their use of ICT in classroom practice*. Doctoral thesis. Open University.

Beauchamp, C., and Thomas, L. (2009) 'Understanding Teacher Identity: An Overview of Issues in the Literature and Implications for Teacher Education', *Cambridge Journal of Education*, 39(2), pp. 175–189.

Beijaard, D., Meijer, P. C., and Verloop, N. (2004) 'Reconsidering Research on Teachers' Professional Identity', *Teaching and Teacher Education*, 20(2), pp. 107–128.

Beijaard, D., Verloop, N., and Vermunt, J. D. (1999) 'Teachers' Perceptions of Professional Identity: An Exploratory Study from a Personal Knowledge Perspective', *Teaching and Teacher Education*, 1, pp. 749–764.

Bourdieu, P. (1986) 'The Forms of Capital', in Richardson, J. (ed.) *Handbook of Theory and Research for the Sociology of Education*. Connecticut: Greenwood Press, pp. 241–256.

Bronfenbrenner, U. (2009) *The Ecology of Human Development: Experiments by Nature and Design*. Cambridge, Massachusetts: Harvard University Press.

Chang-Kredl, S., and Kingsley, S. (2014) 'Identity Expectations in Early Childhood Teacher Education: Pre-service Teachers' Memories of Prior Experiences and Reasons for Entry into the Profession', *Teaching and Teacher Education*, 43, pp. 27–36.

Durrant, J. (2019) *Teacher Agency, Professional Development and School Improvement*. London: Routledge.

Esteban-Guitart, M., and Moll, L. (2014) 'Funds of Identity: A New Concept Based on the Funds of Knowledge Approach', *Culture and Psychology*, 20(1), pp. 31–48.

Garfinkel, H. (1967) *Studies in Ethnomethodology*. New Jersey: Prentice Hall.

Grayling, A. (2011) 'Psychology: How we Form Beliefs', *Nature*, 474, pp. 446–447.

Hamachek, D. (1999) 'Effective Teachers: What They Do, How They Do It, and the Importance of Self-Knowledge', in Lipka, Richard P. and Brinthaupt, Thomas M. (eds.) *The Role of Self in Teacher Development*. New York: State University of New York Press. pp. 189-224.

Hargreaves, A. (2000) 'Four Ages of Professionalism and Professional Learning', *Teachers and Teaching: Theory and Practice*, 6(2), pp. 151–182.

Korthagen, F. A. J. (2004) 'In Search of the Essence of a Good Teacher: Towards a More Holistic Approach in Teacher Education', *Teaching and Teacher Education*, 20(1), pp. 77–97.

Lave, J. (1988) *Cognition in Practice: Mind, Mathematics, and Culture in Everyday Life*. Cambridge: Cambridge University Press.

Lave, J., and Wenger, E. (1991) *Situated Learning: Legitimate Peripheral Participation*. Cambridge: Cambridge University Press.

Moll, L., Amanti, C., Neff, D., and Gonzalez, N. (1992) 'Funds of Knowledge for Teaching: Using a Qualitative Approach to Connect Homes and Classrooms', *Theory Into Practice*, 31(2), pp. 132–141.

Nias, J. (1993) 'Changing Times, Changing Identities: Grieving for a lost self', in Burgess, R. G. (ed.) *Educational Research and Evaluation: For Policy and Practice?* London: The Falmer Press, pp. 139–156.

Olsen, B. (2008) 'Introducing Teacher Identity and This Volume', *Teacher Education Quarterly*, 35(3), pp. 3–4.

Pillen, M. T., Den Brok, P. J., and Beijaard, D. (2013) 'Profiles and Change in Beginning Teachers' Professional Identity Tensions', *Teaching and Teacher Education*, 34, pp. 86–97.

Priestley, M., Biesta, G., and Robinson, S. (2015) *Teacher Agency: An Ecological Approach*. London: Bloomsbury.

Rogers, C., and Scott, K. (2008) 'The Development of the Personal Self and Professional Identity in Learning to Teach', in Cochran-Smith, M. et al. (eds.) *Handbook of Research on Teacher Education: Enduring Questions and Changing Contexts*. New York: Routledge, pp. 732–755.

Rokeach, M. (1985) 'Inducing Change and Stability in Belief Systems and Personality Structures', *Journal of Social Issues*, 41(1), pp. 153–171.

Twining, P., Browne, N. et al. (2017) *NP3: New Purposes, New Practices, New Pedagogy: Meta-analysis Report*. London: Society for Educational Studies. http://edfutures.net/images/e/e7/NP3_Meta-analysis_report.pdf

Usó-Doménech, J. L., and Nescolarde-Selva, J. (2016) 'What are Belief Systems?', *Foundations of Science*, 21(1), pp. 147–152.

Vélez-Ibáñez, C. G., and Greenberg, J. B. (1992) 'Formation and Transformation of Funds of Knowledge among U.S. Mexican Households', *Anthropology & Education Quarterly*, 23(4), pp. 313–335.

CHAPTER

6 Probing your practice

In previous chapters of this book, we have unpacked pedagogical terminology (Chapter 3), explored different Pedagogical Beliefs (Chapter 4), and taken you through a process of unpacking what influences your own practice (Chapter 5). Our main focus thus far has been on helping you to more precisely understand your own individual Pedagogical Beliefs.

However, beliefs are intangible. Beliefs only become tangible through communication (what we say) and action (what we do). This becomes problematic if we want to be precise because as human beings, what we consciously believe, what we say, what we intend to do, what we live out through our actions, and what we implicitly believe are often subtly different (Tannen et al., 2015; Rogers et al., 2005).

Historically, when discussing classroom practice or professional learning there is a tendency to assume these different aspects are always perfectly aligned.

However, if we want to forefront our Pedagogical Beliefs (as underpinning meaning within our practice), then we are dependent on examination of what we think, say, intend and do. Yet, if what we intend to do (Pedagogical Intentions) and what we do (Enacted Practice) are not aligned, then this suggests that the beliefs underpinning our Intended Practice are not aligned with the beliefs underpinning our Enacted Practice (which tend to align with our Implicit beliefs).

The purpose of this chapter is to identify the level of alignment between what you plan to do (Intended Practice), what you actually do (Enacted Practice), and your Implicit Beliefs.

DOI: 10.4324/9781003321637-6

Terminology and alignment

To help surface the level of precision required for meaningful consideration of Pedagogical Beliefs, we are using some specific terms:

- espoused
- conscious
- intended
- enacted
- implicit
- experienced
- outcomes.

Let's look at each of these in turn. Then we will look at what we need to consider if we want to make adjustments to any of them.

The term **espoused** is used to refer to the Pedagogical Beliefs that we talk about; our spoken views about teaching, learning, knowledge, and the purpose or goal of school. These views can be overarching or about specific instances of practice, and aspects of our practice may be used to exemplify a point that we are trying to make. Our espousal may contain words that can be taken literally, as well as spoken or written words that contain specific meaning through the choice of terminology (e.g. when we use particular phrases to align ourselves with particular audiences or trends – such as retrieval practice or deep dives). What we espouse is usually consciously defined (i.e. we think about the overarching message we want to convey before speaking or writing). It is often dependent upon what discourse analysis calls Dialogic Undertones – meaning that a speaker assumes that an understanding is shared by both the speaker and the audience based on previous interactions (Hodges, 2015). We don't necessarily think through every specific word or phrase that we use when communicating with others, but we may consciously choose specific terminology in order to communicate more effectively with a particular audience (Bourdieu & Wacquant, 1992). However, it is unlikely that we analyse the impact of every single word that we use – much of our word choice is simply an embedded part of our everyday vocabulary reflecting the environment that we have emerged from (Bernstein, 1971).

Pedagogical Beliefs can be conscious or implicit. The term **Conscious Beliefs** is used to refer to beliefs that are conscious. These are the beliefs that we recognise that we have. We can espouse them and use them to inform our intentions. The term **Implicit Beliefs** is used to refer to beliefs that we are not aware of. Surfacing our Implicit Beliefs can be problematic because sometimes we consciously think we believe one thing (Conscious Belief), but when we reflect on our practice and the subliminal messages embedded within it, the evidence sometimes suggests that we might implicitly believe something slightly different.

Sometimes we become aware of this ourselves, but more often we become aware of it as a result of interactions with other people. Another person's interpretation of what is implicit within our actions may be different to our own interpretation. This is why gentle coaching and reflective conversations can be such powerful instruments in helping us to understand our Implicit Beliefs.

The term **Pedagogical Intention** is used to refer to what we intend to do – our intended Pedagogical Practices. These intentions can be either specific to an instance of practice (e.g. practical actions within a specific lesson) or broader intentions about practice (e.g. an approach to be adopted over a period of time). Conscious Beliefs and broad intentions are very similar. However, it is helpful to think of beliefs as ideologically oriented and broad intentions as logistically oriented. In other words, once something moves from being an idea to a tangible plan, it shifts from being a belief to an intention. Pedagogical Intentions should not be confused with intended learning outcomes (see the following definition of outcomes).

The term **enacted** is used to refer to actions which are actually carried out and which could be observed. Enacted practice is always specific to a precise moment in time and is therefore a past event (actions due to be enacted in the future would be considered as Intended Practice). Sometimes, people refer to classroom actions as 'actual practice' or 'reality'. However, this is rather problematic because 'actual' or 'reality' suggests that events can be viewed completely objectively – that there is only one 'true' way of seeing something. This view assumes what researchers refer to as a positivistic lens (Cohen et al., 2018). However, our actions may be interpreted differently depending on who is observing or analysing them. For example, the teacher themself may have one view about what happened, their line manager may have another view, and each of their learners may have other views. From an interpretivist perspective, there is therefore not a single 'reality' but instead multiple interpretations and, thus, multiple realities. This is important to remember when we talk about refining future practice based on an interpretation of today's practice. These subjective realities (interpretations) affect where we focus future changes or refinements and define whose insights influence future aspirations and goals.

The term **experienced** is used to refer to what someone (e.g. learners) experiences through our practice. It is a form of interpretation – separating out what we think happened (our own reflection) from what others think happened (their experience). This distinction is important because regardless of what we say, intend, or believe, it is what is experienced by our learners which determines their learning outcomes.

When we talk about **learning outcomes**, these may be intended (what we want the learners to learn), or they may be achieved (what a learner actually learnt). It is important to differentiate between Pedagogical Intentions (what we plan to do through our Pedagogical Practices) and learning outcomes (what has been or is intended to be learnt by our learners).

We are now going to take you through three guided activities which will focus your attention on the relationship between the Pedagogical Beliefs underpinning your Pedagogical Intentions and Enacted Practice. (It is beyond the scope of this book to unpack how your learners each experience your practice because that would require a detailed unpacking of each learner's Funnels of Influence).

This sequence of guided activities works a bit like peeling an onion a layer at a time, so it is important that you complete all parts of each activity and that you do so in order. The most valuable part of these activities will be reflecting back on your findings, so it is important that you use the spaces provided to make notes.

Guided Activity 6.1: Unpacking intended practice

Purpose: To identify which pedagogical stance your Intended Practice aligns with.

Time needed: 1 hour

- Step 1: Unpacking Intended Practice
- Step 2: Identifying the Pedagogical Beliefs that underpin your Intended Practice
- Step 3: Identifying which pedagogical stance your Intended Practice aligns with

We strongly recommend you use the editable version of this Guided Activity, which you can download from www.onelifelearning.co.uk/resources

It is very hard to unpack your own practice effectively in isolation rather than as a coached activity. The nature of the unpacking requires an open mind and a willingness to consider ideas and perspectives that you may not necessarily have considered before. If you are able to work through this with another person to support you as part of a coaching activity, this would be useful. Much of the value of this activity will come from the metacognition involved in carrying out the activity process itself.

Step 1: Unpacking intended practice

We are going to focus on your intentions for the use of digital technology.

First, choose a learning activity that you are about to teach – one that you have already planned and in which your learners will be using some form of digital technology. This should be a typical activity – it should not be 'out of the ordinary' for your teaching. (Note: it needs to be a learning activity that has not yet taken place so that the focus is on your intentions rather than reflections on Enacted Practice – we explore that later).

Fill in the following table about your intentions for this particular activity. You may want to focus on one specific group of learners rather than the whole class when responding to the questions. Aim to include as much detail as possible.

Learners	
Describe the learners that you are focusing on for this activity. - Which learners, and why? - How are learners organised, and why? - Which learners will you interact with the most, and why?	
Describe what digital technology will be being used. - Which devices will be used, and by whom? - Which software will be used, and why was it chosen? - How is the digital technology supporting learners – individually and/or collectively?	
Describe what the learners will be doing, including how they are using digital technology. - What will they do? - What will motivate them? - How much choice will learners have about what they do, how they do it, or who they do it with? - Will each learner create their own version, or will the outcome be a group one?	

Purpose	
What are the intended learning outcomes for this activity? - What will change, or be produced? - What will learners be able to do after this activity that they may not have been able to do before?	
How do the intended learning outcomes relate to the overall purpose of schooling? - How will this activity make a difference to the learner in both the short term and the long term?	
View of the teacher	
What will you (the teacher) be doing? (Be as specific and detailed as possible.) - In preparation for the activity? - At the start of the activity? - During the activity? - After the activity?	
What is your intended role in supporting these learners? How would you describe what you do in a short phrase or sentence?	

Rationale	
Explain why you have planned the activity in the way that you described earlier. - Who or what defined what you will be covering in this activity? - How does this activity relate to other activities/lessons? - What has come before this activity? - What milestones, goals, aspirations, or targets does this activity relate to?	

Step 2: Identifying the pedagogical beliefs that underpin your intended practice

In Step 1 of this activity (Activity 6.1) you have *described* your Intended Practice. The next step is to start to unpack the Pedagogical Beliefs that *underpin* your Intended Practice.

We have provided a summary of the four main pedagogical stances in Table 6.1. This means that you can compare your Intended Practice with a set of statements in order to see which stance you most closely align with. It is a lot easier to work through this process if you can see both your Step 1 responses and Table 6.1 at the same time – this will make the comparison process easier. Therefore, if you have not already done so, we suggest that you download the editable and printable versions of these documents from www.onelifelearning.co.uk/resources

Start by looking at your Step 1 responses in the section headed 'Learners'. Then, read the descriptors in Table 6.1 in the section marked Views of Learners and Learning – which of the Table 6.1 descriptors is the closest match for your Step 1 responses? Highlight *one* descriptor in each row that you feel is the closest match.

Continue to compare your responses in Step 1 with the descriptors in Table 6.1. Many of the considerations span more than one of the dimensions of pedagogy (rows), and so you will need to compare and contrast across rows in order to find a best fit.

Remember, it is not possible to pick and choose parts of a theory – so if you find that more than one descriptor could apply, think critically and be prepared to revisit and refine your responses. It is important to remain open-minded and mitigate any form of bias – such as the Ostrich Effect, ignoring discomfort; Confirmation Bias, seeking affirmation; or Cherry-Picking, artificial filtering (Aubrey-Smith, 2020).

You can only select **one descriptor in each row**.

Table 6.1 Summary of the four main pedagogical stances

Purpose of education	**Traditional**	**Individual Constructivist**	**Social Constructivist**	**Sociocultural**
The purpose of education is to …	imbue learners with habits, rules, procedures, and knowledge that have been predefined as being important for the functioning of society.	help learners develop organised, abstract mental models of the world, and procedures for applying them which are transferable across situations.	help learners develop organised, abstract mental models of the world, and procedures for applying them which are transferable across situations. Learners need to understand the nature of subject domains and the ways in which their knowledge bases are socially constructed.	support learners in becoming competent in valued social practices, within a range of different communities each of which has its own shared objectives and valued ways of working.
Views of Learners and Learning	**Traditional**	**Individual Constructivist**	**Social Constructivist**	**Sociocultural**
Learners are …	seen as empty vessels who learn through imitation or acquisition.	active constructors of their knowledge.	active co-constructors of their knowledge.	seen as active and agentive. They have multiple identities and competencies, each linked to the different communities they belong to.
Learning is …	an individual activity that involves receiving information that the learner can recall when needed.	an individual activity that involves integrating new information into their existing individual mental model.	reliant on dialogue to co-construct understanding, which becomes part of the individuals' existing mental models.	an appropriation of social understandings within particular communities – it is about identity formation (becoming) and participation (belonging) that involves mutually agreeing meaning through interaction.

(Continued)

Table 6.1 (Continued)

View of teachers and teaching	Traditional	Individual constructivist	Social constructivist	Sociocultural
Learning potential is …	determined by a learner's innate abilities.	limited by a learner's age or stage of development – initially their mental models are of specific representations of particular instances of a phenomenon (concrete representations), which at a later stage will become abstract models that can be applied across contexts.	not limited by age or stage but by the sophistication of the learners' existing models and the experiences that they have had.	dependent on the experiences they have had within the communities they belong to.
Motivation is …	extrinsic – through rewards, punishments, pace, and competition.	intrinsic – learners want to make sense of the world and resolve inconsistencies within their mental models – as such they are self-directed and self-regulated.	intrinsic – learners want to make sense of how others in society see the world.	intrinsic – learners want to belong to particular communities and be recognised as valued members of them.

(Continued)

View of teachers and teaching	Traditional	Individual constructivist	Social constructivist	Sociocultural
Teachers are seen as …	the holders of knowledge.	facilitators who create the conditions needed for learning.	knowledgeable about different subject domains and how to direct learning.	knowledgeable in socially valued ways of working.
The role of the teacher is to …	instruct.	guide learning.	scaffold learning.	orchestrate support available to learners.
Teaching involves …	breaking information down into small sequential steps, using strategies such as drill and practice, and enhancing motivation through the pace of the lesson, introducing competition, and using other forms of reward (and punishment).	introducing new information that does not align with the learner's existing mental model – which in turn leads to learning (re-organising of that mental model to resolve cognitive conflict). Making meaning is an individual process. However, cooperation with others can create cognitive conflict, the resolution of which leads to learning.	engaging learners in collaboration with others - through reconciling their different mental models, learning occurs. Where interaction is with someone (e.g. a peer or teacher) who knows more about the subject than the learner does, the learner can achieve more than they would be able to achieve on their own – working in this space is known as the 'Zone of Proximal Development' (Vygotsky, 1978).	connecting classroom activities to valued practices in the world and making meanings explicit for learners to use.

(Continued)

Table 6.1 (Continued)

View of knowledge	Traditional	Individual constructivist	Social constructivist	Sociocultural
What is knowledge?	Knowledge is a representation of how the world actually is.	Knowledge is an individual's mental representation of the world – how the world is perceived to be by the individual.	Knowledge is a social construction – not an objective reality.	Knowledge is the ability to act in meaningful ways within particular communities, which have shared goals and shared valued ways of working.
Knowledge and context	Knowledge is explicit. Words, and other symbols such as numbers, carry meaning, which is stable across contexts and learners.	Knowledge is explicit and can be transferred across contexts.	Knowledge is socially constructed and so dependent on context.	Knowledge is explicit or tacit but is always situated in particular communities.
How does knowledge relate to an individual?	Knowledge is an acquired property of an individual.	Knowledge is an individually constructed property of an individual.	Knowledge is socially co-constructed through dialogue and individually acquired.	Knowledge is created through activity and possessed by individuals and groups.

Adapted from Murphy's Innovative Pedagogy Framework
Patricia Murphy - https://halfbaked.education/murphys-innovative-pedagogy-framework/

Step 3: Identifying which pedagogical stance your intended practice aligns with

Look at the descriptors which you have highlighted in Table 6.1. Which pedagogical stance (see column headings) does this suggest that your Intended Practice most closely aligns with (circle **one**):

Traditional	Individual Constructivist	Social Constructivist	Sociocultural

Guided Activity 6.2: Identifying which pedagogical stance your enacted practice aligns with

Purpose: To identify which Pedagogical Stance your Enacted Practice aligns with.
Time needed: 2 hours (including implementing a learning activity)

- Step 1: Unpacking your Enacted Practice
- Step 2: Identifying the Pedagogical Beliefs that underpin your Enacted Practice
- Step 3: Identifying which pedagogical stance your Enacted Practice aligns with

We strongly recommend you use the editable version of this Guided Activity, which you can download from www.onelifelearning.co.uk/resources

Step 1: Unpacking your enacted practice

At this point you need to carry out the activity that you have described in Activity 6.1. Please do not attempt to continue this Guided activity until you have done so.

Once you have enacted that practice, continue with this guided activity by filling in the table provided here to describe what was enacted.

Make sure that you focus on the same specific group of learners that you described in Activity 6.1 Step 1.

Whilst the questions are very similar to the ones in Activity 6.1 Step 1, this time you will be noting down what you *actually* did rather than what you *intended* to do. You may find that your answers are very similar to your responses in Activity 6.1 Step 1, or you may find that what 'actually happened' was subtly different from what was intended. For most people, there will be differences – which reflect the wide range of influences that affect us in each Moment of Practice.

Learners	
Describe the learners that you focused on for this activity. - Which learners, and why? - How were learners organised, and why? - Which learners did you interact with the most, and why?	
Describe what digital technology was used. - Which devices were used, and by whom? - Which software was used, and why was it chosen? - How was the digital technology supporting learners – individually and/or collectively?	
Describe what the learners did, including how they used digital technology. - What did they do? - What motivated the learners? - How much choice did learners have about what they did, how they did it, or who they did it with? - Did each learner create their own version, or was the outcome a group one?	

Purpose	
What learning outcomes were achieved? - What changed or was produced? - What were learners able to do after this activity that they had not been able to do before?	
How do the achieved learning outcomes relate to the overall purpose of schooling? - How did this activity make a difference to the learner – thinking about both the short term and the long term?	
View of the teacher	
What did you (the teacher) do? (Be as specific and detailed as possible.) - In preparation for the activity? - At the start of the activity? - During the activity? - After the activity?	

What was your role in supporting these learners? How would you describe what you did in a short phrase or sentence?	
Rationale	
Explain why the activity took place in the way that you described earlier. - Who or what were any expected or unexpected influences affecting this activity? - How did you respond to those influences? For example, what did you say/do/prioritise/change? Why did you make those decisions?	

Step 2: Identifying the pedagogical beliefs that underpin your enacted practice

In Step 1 of this activity, you *described* your Enacted Practice. The next step is to start to unpack the Pedagogical Beliefs that underpin your Enacted practice. This process works exactly the same as Activity 6.1 Step 2 where you compared your Intended Practice to Table 6.1.

We have provided another copy of the four main pedagogical stances in Table 6.2. Compare your Enacted Practice with this set of statements in order to see which stance your practice most closely aligns with. Highlight one descriptor that you feel is closest match in each row. Remember that you can only select one descriptor in each row – so if you find that more than one descriptor could apply, think critically and be prepared to revisit and refine your responses. It is important to remain open-minded.

Table 6.2 Summary of the four main pedagogical stances

Purpose of education	**Traditional**	**Individual constructivist**	**Social constructivist**	**Sociocultural**
The purpose of education is to …	imbue learners with habits, rules, procedures, and knowledge that have been predefined as being important for the functioning of society.	help learners develop organised, abstract mental models of the world and procedures for applying them which are transferable across situations.	help learners develop organised, abstract mental models of the world and procedures for applying them which are transferable across situations. Learners need to understand the nature of subject domains and the ways in which their knowledge bases are socially constructed.	support learners in becoming competent in valued social practices, within a range of different communities each of which has its own shared objectives and valued ways of working.
Views of learners and learning	**Traditional**	**Individual constructivist**	**Social constructivist**	**Sociocultural**
Learners are …	seen as empty vessels who learn through imitation or acquisition.	active constructors of their knowledge.	active co-constructors of their knowledge.	seen as active and agentive. They have multiple identities and competencies, each linked to the different communities they belong to.

(Continued)

Table 6.2 (Continued)

Views of learners and learning	Traditional	Individual constructivist	Social constructivist	Sociocultural
Learning is …	an individual activity that involves receiving information that the learner can recall when needed.	an individual activity that involves integrating new information into their existing individual mental model.	reliant on dialogue to co-construct understanding, which becomes part of the individuals' existing mental models.	an appropriation of social understandings within particular communities – it is about identity formation (becoming) and participation (belonging) that involves mutually agreeing on meaning through interaction.
Learning potential is …	determined by a learner's innate abilities.	limited by a learner's age or stage of development – initially their mental models are of specific representations of particular instances of a phenomenon (concrete representations), which, at a later stage, will become abstract models that can be applied across contexts.	not limited by age or stage but by the sophistication of the learners' existing models and the experiences that they have had.	dependent on the experiences they have had within the communities they belong to.
Motivation is . ..	extrinsic – through rewards, punishments, pace, and competition.	intrinsic – learners want to make sense of the world and to resolve inconsistencies within their mental models – as such they are self-directed and self-regulated.	intrinsic – learners want to make sense of how others in society see the world.	intrinsic – learners want to belong to particular communities and be recognised as valued members of them.

(*Continued*)

View of teachers and teaching	Traditional	Individual constructivist	Social constructivist	Sociocultural
Teachers are seen as …	the holders of knowledge.	facilitators who create the conditions needed for learning.	knowledgeable about different subject domains and how to direct learning.	knowledgeable in socially valued ways of working.
The role of the teacher is to …	instruct.	guide learning.	scaffold learning.	orchestrate support available to learners.
Teaching involves …	breaking information down into small sequential steps, using strategies such as drill and practice, and enhancing motivation through the pace of the lesson, introducing competition, and using other forms of reward (and punishment).	introducing new information that does not align with the learner's existing mental model – which, in turn, leads to learning (re-organising of that mental model to resolve cognitive conflict). Making meaning is an individual process. However, cooperation with others can create cognitive conflict, the resolution of which leads to learning.	engaging learners in collaboration with others – through reconciling their different mental models, learning occurs. Where interaction is with someone (e.g. a peer or teacher) who knows more about the subject than the learner does, the learner can achieve more than they would be able to achieve on their own – this is known as the 'Zone of Proximal Development (Vygotsky, 1978).	connecting classroom activities to valued practices in the world and making meanings explicit for learners to use.

(*Continued*)

Table 6.2 (Continued)

View of knowledge	Traditional	Individual constructivist	Social constructivist	Sociocultural
What is knowledge?	Knowledge is a representation of how the world actually is.	Knowledge is an individual's mental representation of the world – how the world is perceived to be by the individual.	Knowledge is a social construction – not an objective reality.	Knowledge is the ability to act in meaningful ways within particular communities, which have shared goals and shared valued ways of working.
Knowledge and context	Knowledge is explicit. Words, and other symbols such as numbers, carry meaning, which is stable across contexts and learners.	Knowledge is explicit and can be transferred across contexts.	Knowledge is socially constructed and so dependent on context.	Knowledge is explicit or tacit but is always situated in particular communities.
How does knowledge relate to an individual?	Knowledge is an acquired property of an individual.	Knowledge is an individually constructed property of an individual.	Knowledge is socially co-constructed through dialogue and individually acquired.	Knowledge is created through activity and possessed by individuals and groups.

Adapted from Murphy's Innovative Pedagogy Framework
Patricia Murphy – https://halfbaked.education/murphys-innovative-pedagogy-framework/

Step 3: Identifying which pedagogical stance your enacted practice aligns with

Look at the descriptors which you have highlighted in Table 6.2.

Which pedagogical stance (see column headings) does this suggest that your Enacted Practice most closely aligns with (circle **one**):

Traditional	Individual Constructivist	Social Constructivist	Sociocultural

Guided Activity 6.3: Comparing alignment between your intended and enacted practice

Purpose: To explore the pedagogical stances underpinning your Intended and Enacted Practice
Time: 30 minutes

- Step 1: Comparing beliefs underpinning Enacted and Intended Practice
- Step 2: Reflecting on the alignment between Intended and Enacted Practice

We strongly recommend you use the editable version of this Guided Activity, which you can download from www.onelifelearning.co.uk/resources

Step 1: Comparing beliefs underpinning enacted and intended practice

We are now going to compare the pedagogical stance embedded within your Intended Practice (from Activity 6.1 Step 3) with the pedagogical stance underpinning your Enacted Practice (from Guided Activity 6.2 Step 3).

By examining this alignment, we can surface the extent to which the beliefs underpinning your Intended Practice align with those underpinning your Enacted Practice.

In Activity 6.1, Step 3 **the beliefs underpinning my Intended Practice** aligned with: *(Circle one)*	Traditional Individual Constructivist Social Constructivist Sociocultural
In Activity 6.2, Step 3 **the beliefs underpinning my Enacted Practice** aligned with: *(Circle one)*	Traditional Individual Constructivist Social Constructivist Sociocultural
Conclusion To what extent are *the beliefs underpinning your Intended Practice* (from Activity 6.1 Step 3) aligned with the beliefs underpinning your Enacted Practice (from Activity 6.2 Step 3)?	

Step 2: Reflecting on the alignment between Intended and enacted practice

We are now going to spend some time reflecting on the relationship between your Intended and Enacted Practice and the beliefs underpinning them. This kind of critical reflection can be very difficult to do on your own. This is because we are more used to evaluative reflection where we are motivated to see alignment between our Intended and Enacted Practice because judgements are being made about our capabilities. However, in the context of this book you are encouraged to reflect more critically and more deeply – aiming to avoid potential confirmation bias – where we only see what we go looking for (Hattie & Hamilton, 2020).

It is helpful to remind ourselves that this activity is about unpacking and analysing rather than evaluating and forming judgements.

Reflection A My Enacted Practice differed from my Intended Practice *because …*	*(e.g. my Enacted Practice probably aligned more with xxx because I prioritised zzz in the classroom.)*

Reflection B What did you notice or learn through the *process* of doing this comparison?	*(e.g. When I compared my responses to the Pedagogy Framework, I 'wanted' my Enacted Practice to align with xxx, but I think it probably aligns more with yyy.)*
Reflection C What do you think **affected any differences** between your Intended Practice and your Enacted Practice? Think back to the Funnels of Influence (Chapter 5) – you may find it helpful to revisit Guided Activity 5.1 before responding to this Reflection.	*(e.g. I probably prioritised xxx because my childhood teacher did xxx and it made me think xxx. In my school today the culture is yyy which means that zzz.)*

The purpose of this task is to help you become more aware of the alignment or misalignment between the beliefs underpinning your Intended Practice and Enacted Practice. This helps surface any inconsistency between what you Consciously and Implicitly believe. This is because our Enacted Practice is often a clearer reflection of our Implicit Beliefs than our Intended Practice, which is often more aligned with our Conscious Beliefs. Therefore, if there is a lack of alignment between our Intended Practice and our Enacted Practice, it is likely to be because our Implicit Beliefs conflict with our Conscious Beliefs.

Conclusion

This chapter has taken you on a journey where you have explicitly identified the Pedagogical Beliefs that your Intended and Enacted Practice appear to align with. By doing so, you will have surfaced the extent of alignment between your Conscious and Implicit Pedagogical Beliefs.

Ultimately, we should be aiming for our Implicit Pedagogical Beliefs to be reflected in our Conscious Pedagogical Beliefs. In turn, we should aim for our Conscious Beliefs to be reflected and achieved through our Intended and Enacted Practice. However, such perfect alignment rarely exists due to the many influences that affect us.

We refer to the variance between beliefs, intentions, and practice as the Pedagogical Alignment Gap, and whilst it may always exist in some form, we can, and should, attempt to reduce it.

Closing the Pedagogical Alignment Gap is vitally important because of the significant impact that this has on our learners. In Chapter 2, we introduced the pivotal role that our childhood teachers have on forming our learner identity. In Chapter 5, we introduced the deeply rooted way that formative experiences shape the lens with which we grow up to see and understand the world around us. If we are providing inconsistent or misaligned messages to our learners, we create confusion and barriers to their understanding of the following:

- What it means to be a learner and to learn
- What it means to be an educator and to educate others
- What knowledge is and how it is formed
- What the role and purpose of schooling is

In Chapter 8, we discuss the Pedagogical Alignment Gap in more detail. Before we do that, we are going to explore the different ways in which the same digital technology can be used effectively by people who have different pedagogical stances.

References

Aubrey-Smith, F., (2020) 'Interventions: How Well Do You Know Your Cognitive Bias?' *SecEd*, 5 February 2020.

Bernstein, B., (1971) *Class, Codes and Control.* London: Routledge.

Bourdieu, P., and Wacquant, L. J. D. (1992) *An Invitation to Reflexive Sociology.* Chicago: University of Chicago Press.

Cohen, L., Manion, L., and Morrison, K., (2018) *Research Methods in Education.* 8th edn. London: Routledge.

Hattie, J., and Hamilton, A. (2020) *Why We Focus on the Wrong Drivers in Education.* London: Sage Publications Ltd.

Hodges, A. (2015) 'Intertextuality in Discourse', in Tannen, D., Hamilton, H. E., and Schiffrin, D. (eds) *The Handbook of Discourse Analysis.* 2nd edn. US: Wiley-Blackwell. pp.42–60.

Rogers, R. et al. (2005) 'Critical Discourse Analysis in Education: A Review of the Literature', *Review of Educational Research*, 75(3), pp. 365–416.

Tannen, D. et al. (2015) *The Handbook of Discourse Analysis.* 2nd edn. Chichester: Blackwell.

Vygotsky, L. (1978) *Mind in Society: Development of Higher Psychological Processes.* Cambridge MA: Harvard University Press.

CHAPTER

7

What kinds of tech use for what kind of pedagogy?

There has been notable worldwide reflection on the role of digital technology to support teaching and learning (e.g. ESC, 2022). As set out at the beginning of this book, quantitative evidence shows a sustained increase in levels of financial investment by schools from 2018 to 2022 (e.g. IMARC, 2022; EEE, 2021). Additionally, both qualitative and quantitative research has shown that more teachers and leaders now see digital technology as a vital tool to support learning (e.g. OUP, 2022; OECD, 2022; UNESCO, 2021).

Amongst all of this, conversations globally with schools show that despite financial investment and a belief in the role of digital technology, many colleagues are still not quite sure what digital technology to use and how to use it or are looking to see more impact from existing investments.

From your own experience, you will already know that different teachers use digital technology in different ways. It is often assumed that this is because of different levels of digital skills or to do with available equipment, personal interest or enthusiasm in using digital technology. However, as you will have discovered through earlier chapters of this book, that is only part of the story – a big influence comes from our Pedagogical Beliefs and thus different views on the relevance of particular tools and resources.

Guided Activity 7.1: Your use of digital technology

Purpose: To clarify your beliefs about digital technology and to compare them with your Enacted Practice when using digital technology in your teaching.

Time needed: 45 minutes

- Step 1: Your Conscious Beliefs about digital technology
- Step 2: Your use of digital technology in your Pedagogical Practice

DOI: 10.4324/9781003321637-7

We strongly recommend you use the editable version of this Guided Activity, which you can download from www.onelifelearning.co.uk/resources.

Step 1: Your conscious beliefs about digital technology

Let's think about your Conscious Beliefs about digital technology.

We are asking you to think specifically about how you explain your rationale for using digital technology within teaching and learning. The following questions will seem very similar but should draw out subtle but important aspects of your beliefs about digital technology.

Note down your responses after each question.

What benefits or features of digital technology do you usually talk about?
I think that digital technology is useful because ...

How do you describe the educational contribution made by digital technology?
I plan for my learners to use digital technology because ...

How have you previously described the relationship between digital technology and learning?
I think that digital technology enhances the way that learning is supported by ...

Step 2: Your use of digital technology in your pedagogical practice

Now think about how you use digital technology in your teaching.

Think back over the last couple of weeks of teaching and fill in the following table.

- In the left-hand column, list the digital technology that was used in your lessons.
- In the right-hand column, make notes about how that digital technology was used – include information about who was using it and how they were using it.

What digital technology was used?	How was that digital technology used? What impact do you think this had?

We are now going to unpack these ideas.

Digital technology frameworks

Digital technology frameworks can be helpful in supporting our thinking about how to use digital technology and what impact it may have.

Twining (2008) identified five categories of frameworks which provide a lens for thinking about digital technology in education. These are achievement frameworks, cognitive frameworks, software frameworks, pedagogical frameworks, and evolutionary frameworks. Pedagogical frameworks are the most important when you are thinking about how to use digital technology in education because of the importance of ensuring coherent experiences for your learners.

Cherner and Mitchell (2021), in their evaluation of frameworks for supporting digital technology use, highlight the importance of being a critical user of any framework – considering its intention, design, and origins. This is a particular challenge for those of us interested in digital technology in schools because there is a history of frameworks that steer us towards a kind of compliance mindset. In other words, frameworks in which the desirable outcomes are ones that their authors perceive as 'good practice' – which may or may not align with our own views (e.g. Christodoulou, 2020; NAACE, 2018; EEF, 2019).

As an example, let's think about one of the pedagogical frameworks most commonly used by schools (at the time of writing) to support the use of digital technology; Puentedura's (2010) Substitution, Augmentation, Modification, and Redefinition (SAMR) framework. SAMR consists of four hierarchical levels of use of digital technology that teachers should aspire to work progressively through (see Table 7.1).

The SAMR framework is widely adopted and cited by those who find appeal in its accessible nature, and the ambiguity of the level descriptors is attractive to those who seek to utilise it to stimulate discussion (Aldosemani, 2019; Moane, 2019). However, these same features result in a lack of precision (Twining, 2008), which creates inconsistent application and impact. It is important to bear in mind that one of the criticisms that SAMR faces is that it was published without theoretical evidence underpinning it. Furthermore, there is a lack of supporting empirical research to justify its claims to make pedagogy more effective. There is an implicit assumption within the SAMR framework that moving from Substitution to Redefinition will result in an improvement, but this would only be true if your Pedagogical Beliefs align with the pedagogical values underpinning the framework. The beliefs underpinning SAMR are implicit, although the framework bears a close resemblance to Dwyer et al.'s (1990) 'Five phase model of teacher development' (see Table 7.1), which was more explicit about how different levels align with different pedagogical stances. Dwyer et al. (1990) highlight that their focus was explicitly biased towards constructivist principles – and that moving from a Traditional pedagogical stance to a Constructivist one was seen as an improvement.

Table 7.1 Dwyer et al.'s (1990) five phase model of teacher development, compared with Substitution, Augmentation, Modification, and Redefinition (SAMR), (Puentedura, 2010)

SAMR **Puentedura (2010)**	**Dwyer et al.'s (1990) five-phase model of teacher development**
Redefinition: 'Tech allows for the creation of new tasks, previously inconceivable.'	**Invention**: Purposeful radical change in classroom practices.
Modification: 'Tech allows for significant task redesign.'	**Appropriation**: Roles shifted noticeably and new instructional patterns emerge – from teacher to facilitator – from didactic to constructivist.
Augmentation: 'Tech acts as a direct tool substitute, with functional improvement.'	**Adaptation**: Increasing student productivity, allowing more time for teachers to engage students in 'higher-order learning objectives' (Dwyer et al., 1990, p. 6).
Substitution: 'Tech acts as a direct tool substitute, with no functional change.'	**Adoption**: Use of new technology to support Traditional model of didactic teaching
	Entry: Traditional schooling, based on didactic models of teaching and 'knowledge transmission', firmly in place

Digital technology frameworks – including SAMR and other well-known examples such as TPACK (Mishra and Koehler, 2006) – are undoubtedly useful in galvanising discussion. However, they suffer from the problem of pedagogical ambiguity and their failure to support teachers in thinking about how different elements within the framework dynamically relate to each other. Whilst the ambiguity and subjective nature of those frameworks is attractive and engaging, its lack of precision perpetuates the issues in EdTech outlined in Chapter 2.

Twining's (2018) Digital Technology Impact Framework (DTIF) not only avoids the problem of favouring one pedagogical stance over another but also shows how key facets of digital technology use interact with each other. The DTIF[1] consists of three main dimensions, the first two of which – as seen in Figure 7.1 - are

- ***Quantity*** relates to the proportion of available learning time that digital technology is being used *by the learners themselves*. This underpins the other two dimensions.
- ***Focus*** categorises the objectives underlying the use of digital technology. If digital technology is not in use, then the Focus dimension does not apply.

The three Focus categories follow:

- ***Learning ABOUT digital technology*** – where the focus is on learning digital technology competencies. This might be referred to in the curriculum as Computing, Computer Science, Digital Skills, Information Communication and Technology (ICT), and the like.
- ***Learning WITH digital technology*** – where the focus is on learning something other than digital technology competencies, for example, using digital technology to enhance your learning about history or science.
- ***Other*** – where the focus is not on learning ABOUT or WITH digital technology. This might include using digital technology as a reward or to occupy learners so that the teacher can focus on supporting other learners.

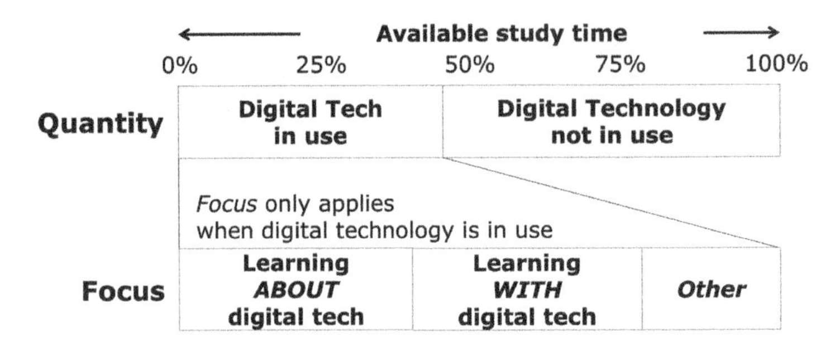

Figure 7.1 Diagrammatic overview of the first two dimensions of the digital technology impact framework (DTIF)

Where the *Focus* is on learning WITH digital technology your Pedagogical Beliefs will guide how you use it and the impact that it can have.

To help illustrate this in practice, we have designed a guided activity which will unpack how digital technology can be used effectively from the perspectives of the four pedagogical stances that we introduced in Chapter 4.

Guided Activity 7.2: Exploring digital technology use

Purpose: To give you:

- practical examples illustrating how and why the same digital technology would be used differently by teachers holding different Pedagogical Beliefs
- a set of practical ideas about how using digital technology in specific ways might align with your own Pedagogical Beliefs

Time required: 60 minutes

- Step 1: Niq's use of digital technology (Traditional Stance)
- Step 2: Sam's use of digital technology (Individual Constructivist Stance)
- Step 3: Aba's use of digital technology (Social Constructivist Stance)
- Step 4: Jo's use of digital technology (Sociocultural Stance)
- Step 5: Reflecting on your own practice

We strongly recommend you use the editable version of this Guided Activity, which you can download from www.onelifelearning.co.uk/resources

The four personas introduced in Chapter 4 – Niq, Sam, Aba, and Jo – each illustrate a different pedagogical stance. We are going to expand the Pedagogical Practice we presented in Chapter 4 to illustrate how each persona might use the same range of digital technology in ways that align with their specific Pedagogical Beliefs.

Some important notes to be aware of as you work through these illustrations:

- Embedded within each example are comments (*shown in italics and in brackets*) that explain how that particular use of digital technology illustrates a specific Pedagogical Belief.
- Not all the identified uses would be likely to be implemented in each example of practice – they are examples that illustrate the sorts of ways in which the teacher might use digital technology.
- We are intentionally focusing on digital technology commonly found across many schools. As a result, it is likely that you will have either used one or more of the following digital technology examples or that you will have seen a colleague do so.
- We are deliberately not looking at what some would consider less commonly used school digital technology such as augmented and virtual reality, wearable technologies, artificial intelligence–powered chatbots, and video gaming.
- We are also avoiding focusing on digital technology that would most commonly be used as part of a computing curriculum such as robots and programmable environments (i.e. where the Focus is on learning ABOUT digital technology).
- Given the contentious nature of using smartphones in schools, we are also not including these pocket-sized computers in our discussions about digital technology used in schools.
- We are also deliberately focusing on digital technology that can be used regularly across lessons in any subject or across any age group of learners in order to maximise the time spent learning WITH digital technology relative to time spent learning ABOUT digital technology.

In Steps 1–4 of this guided activity, you will be taken through typical Pedagogical Practice for each of the personas. As you read these you should highlight aspects which mirror how you use digital technology in your practice.

In Step 5, you will reflect on how your use of digital technology (as noted in Guided Activity 7.1 and highlighted in Guided Activity 7.2 Steps 1–4) aligns with that of the four different pedagogical stances (as illustrated by the four examples of Pedagogical Practice provided in Steps 1–4 below).

Step 1: Niq's use of digital technology (traditional stance)

Remember to highlight aspects of this description that mirror how digital technology is used in your practice.

Niq's classroom is organised with the learners' tables in rows facing the front of the class. Niq uses a seating plan which places learners with special educational needs (including behavioural needs) at the front of the classroom and learners whom Niq trusts to conform with expectations in rows at the back. Niq has a **class set of mobile devices** (e.g. laptops, tablets) that are planned for specific learners to use in each session *(Pedagogical Belief: Teachers are the holders of knowledge who instruct the learners).*

During whole-class inputs, Niq uses a range of **accessibility features** to ensure a fully inclusive classroom. These include automated subtitles when using presentations, audio and video clips as stimuli, and presentation content that takes account of visual impairment and cognitive load. Specific learners in Niq's class have been identified by the special educational needs coordinator as requiring **specific accessibility adaptations** as part of their individual action plans *(Learning potential is determined by a learner's innate abilities).* Niq allows these learners to use pre-agreed features in line with the requirements set out in their action plan throughout the session.

At the beginning of the lesson, Niq goes through a **presentation on the large display board** – located at the front of the classroom by the teacher's desk – which consists of pre-prepared content *(Learning involves acquisition of knowledge from the knowledgeable teacher)*, including **interactive images, film and/or audio clips, website pages, and/or slides** that have been created to engage the learners *(Learning is extrinsically motivated).* Niq will have carefully planned a learning sequence that breaks the topic down into small pieces that are introduced in sequence, one at a time *(Teaching involves breaking information down into small sequential steps).* At intervals throughout the presentation, Niq includes multiple-choice questions. The learners put their hands up to respond to the questions on the large display board, and Niq selects individuals to come up to the board to click on the answer they believe to be correct. The rest of the class watches the **board** to see if the answer is right or wrong. If the answer is correct, Niq then moves on to the next part of the presentation. If it is incorrect, then another learner will be asked to come up and have a go or Niq may go back to work through the material again *(Being able to recall information is evidence of learning having taken place; repetition enhances learning).*

After the input (which lasts approximately a third of the lesson time), Niq gives the learners activities to do which involve applying what has been taught to reinforce it *(Teaching involves using strategies such as drill and practice)* and check that they have understood it. Niq has carefully prepared different activities for different groups of learners who are perceived to be of different abilities. This is in order to differentiate the task so that it is appropriate for the differing ability levels of the learners. Niq has three pre-existing groups of learners (low ability, middle ability, and high ability), with ability defined by recorded attributes such as special educational needs or disabilities *(Learning potential is determined by a learner's innate abilities)*. Niq utilises digital technologies that have clear controls on what learners can use, when and how.

The lower ability learners work individually *(Learning is an individual activity)* using **drill and practice software that takes them through a series of questions** linked to Niq's input. If the learner answers a question correctly, then the software rewards them and they are taken to the next question *(Rewards reinforce learning, which is extrinsically motivated)*. If the learner answers incorrectly then the software presents them with information about the correct answer before moving them on to the next question *(Repetition enhances learning)*. The software uses a learner's responses to ensure that the questions they are asked are at an appropriate level of difficulty *(Low ability learners need more repetition than higher ability learners)*. As they work through the questions, the software shows their score (*Rewards reinforce learning*).

The middle-ability learners work individually *(Learning is an individual activity)* using **adaptive software that presents them with information** that initially recaps what Niq taught in the input *(Repetition enhances learning)*. The software asks the learners questions and, based on their answers, decides what information to provide them with next *(Content should be broken down into small sequential chunks)*. The software introduces new material if the learners respond correctly to the initial questions, extending Niq's input. The software displays how many correct answers the learner has achieved *(Rewards reinforce learning)*, how far the learner has progressed through the material, and how the learner is performing relative to other learners *(Competition is motivating)*.

The high-ability learners are those who Niq thinks will already have learnt what has been taught in the input. These learners use **a website that Niq has pre-selected** in order to find the answer to a set of predetermined questions *(The teacher is knowledgeable and should control access to information)*. Whilst they may work in pairs, each learner will record their answers on the worksheet in their own exercise book *(Learning is an individual activity)*. Niq will collect their answers at the end of the lesson to be marked *(A teacher should check that a learner has learnt the correct content, and reward them accordingly)*.

To motivate the learners Niq provides an extension activity – **watching a video** about the topic – for those learners who finish early *(Motivation is extrinsic)*.

A short while before the lesson ends, Niq will return to a **presentation** to deliver a pre-prepared recap, explain any homework *(Repetition enhances learning)*, and provide closing instructions.

Occasionally, Niq will use **quiz software** towards the end of the lesson to test the children's learning of the material that has been delivered. Where possible learners will respond individually to the questions using a mobile device *(Learning is an individual activity)*. The software plays motivating music and has a countdown timer to encourage rapid responses *(Pace enhances motivation)*. After each question, the correct answer is displayed *(Timely reinforcement enhances learning)*, followed by a leaderboard that shows the learners who have answered the most questions quickly and correctly *(Competition enhances motivation)*. Then the next question is presented. There is no discussion of the questions or answers whilst the quiz is taking place *(Learning is an individual process of acquisition of information)*. When the quiz ends, Niq congratulates the learners with the highest scores *(Praise and competition motivate learners)*.

After the lesson, Niq will identify one or two of the best pieces of finished work – chosen because they are judged to be of a standard appropriate to publish on the **school website or through social media** *(Motivation is extrinsic)*. Niq also reviews the **data dashboard produced by the adaptive learning software** and looks at the individual learners' **quiz** results to receive an overview of the proportion of the class that achieved the lesson's intended outcomes *(Learning is evidenced by the ability to recall information)* and identify any material that he needs to re-present in a subsequent lesson *(Repetition enhances learning)*.

Let's now consider how the same digital technology might be used within an Individual Constructivist pedagogical stance.

Step 2: Sam's use of digital technology (individual constructivist stance)

Remember to highlight aspects of this description that mirror how digital technology is used in your practice.

Sam's classroom has clusters of tables organised into horseshoe shapes where learners are all oriented towards the front of the class. Learners are allocated to a table, based on their current level of competence *(Pedagogical Belief: Learning is limited by the learner's age or stage but, within that, depends on the sophistication of their existing mental model and the extent to which they can resolve cognitive conflict when it arises)*. Sam has a **class set of mobile devices** (e.g. laptops, tablets) that learners can use in each session. Whilst Sam often plans who will be using the mobile devices, learners can ask to use them if they have a good reason for doing so *(Teachers are facilitators who create the conditions needed for learning and guide the learners)*.

Prior to the lesson, Sam may have created **video clips** on how to carry out a particular procedure or an explanation of some specific information. Sam does this in order to free up teacher time during the lesson *(Teachers are facilitators who create the conditions needed for learning)*.

During whole-class inputs, Sam uses a range of **accessibility features** to ensure a fully inclusive classroom. These include automated subtitles when using presentations, audio and video clips as stimuli, and presentation content that takes account of visual impairment and cognitive load. Pre-identified learners in Sam's class are allowed to utilise **accessibility features** for specific tasks such as screen masks, talk-to-text, picture dictionaries, audio recording, and screen magnification. Learners are guided to do so based on what Sam perceives as necessary or useful *(Teachers are facilitators who create the conditions needed for learning)*.

Sam usually starts the lesson with a **presentation** to provide a visual reminder of previous material, instructions for today's tasks and signposting to support materials *(Learning builds upon prior knowledge)*. This will be **projected onto a digital board** from a **laptop** – both of which are usually located at the front of the classroom. Sam might use **interactive images, film or audio clips, website pages, or augmented reality apps** to encourage focused discussion as part of this input *(Discussion can cause cognitive conflict, the resolution of which leads to learning)*. Sam checks the learners' understanding at regular intervals using **a mix of open and closed questions** – asking learners to answer/respond using a range of methods *(Understanding a learner's misconceptions helps the teacher to guide their learning)* including hands-up, thumbs-up/down, think–pair–write *(Cooperation can cause cognitive conflict, the resolution of which leads to learning)*. Sam might set a specific task using **question-and-answer software** to show a question, with real-time anonymised answers shown on screen to help identify misconceptions *(Understanding a learner's misconceptions helps the teacher guide their learning; cognitive conflict leads to learning)*.

Once Sam feels that the majority of the class has understood the main points, each group is given an activity to do to reinforce the teaching input. Learners are encouraged to cooperate with each other, talking about the task *(Cooperation with others can create cognitive conflict, the resolution of which leads to learning)*, and each learner completes their own response *(Learning is an individual activity involving the integration of new information into the individual's existing mental model)*. Sam may direct a group to use **adaptive software that takes them through a series of questions** linked to the current topic, which automatically provides new questions or tasks based on correct answers to the previous question. Learners will work individually. *(Learners are active constructors of their knowledge; learning is an individual activity that involves integrating new information into their existing individual mental model)*. Sam reviews incorrect answers with the learners in order to surface misconceptions and alternative strategies *(Learning involves individual learners in creating their own mental model of the world)*.

Another group of learners may **use the internet to search for information** within the parameters set out by Sam. They will be given specific websites or pages to search and will work individually or in pairs *(Cooperation can lead to cognitive conflict that may lead to learning)* to find and individually record information (e.g. as a **concept map**; *Learning is an individual process*) which will then be handed in. Sam will then assess the extent to which each learner is able to utilise their mental model and what misconceptions they may have *(Knowledge is an individual's representation of the world)*.

Another group of learners may cooperate **to produce a cloud-based digital document** (e.g. slides, a page on the school website, an interactive artefact) or an

interactive image or video or audio clip. Learners may work in pairs or small groups *(Cooperation may lead to cognitive conflict, resolution of which leads to learning)* to produce the document, but each learner's contribution will be clearly identifiable *(Learners individually construct their own mental model)*. Learners share their creations via the class **blog**. Whilst third parties can leave comments (e.g. a 'like', a short comment or some kind of recognition), these are pre-moderated by Sam, and the learners will not be allowed to reply directly to them. Having a real audience is seen as making the work meaningful, but interaction with that real audience is not seen as necessary *(Learning is an individual activity that involves integrating new information into their existing individual mental model; whilst interaction with others can be beneficial, it is not essential)*.

Sam tends to work with one group whilst keeping an overview of what the other learners are doing. Sam tries to elicit any misconceptions that the learners in the group have – and then help correct those misconceptions *(Learning involves resolving cognitive conflicts between an individual's existing mental model and new information)*.

At the end of the lesson, Sam will return to their **presentation** to revisit common misconceptions, reinforce the key points for the learners to understand, recap the sequence of work covered, check the completion of intended learning, and identify what will happen in the next lesson as a consequence of this lesson *(Learning involves integrating new information into their existing individual mental model)*. During this input, Sam will use examples of learners' misconceptions as part of checking understanding *(Learning involves resolving cognitive conflicts between an individual's existing mental model and new information)*.

Sam may use **quiz software** at the start or end of a lesson to gauge learners' understanding of the current topic. Learners will respond individually using mobile devices (e.g. laptops, tablets). After each question, the software displays the correct answer, and Sam leads a discussion about why the other answers are incorrect *(It is important to highlight misconceptions)*. Sam focuses on clarifying an individual learner's understanding and tends to avoid competition between learners *(Learning is intrinsically motivated)*.

After the lesson, Sam reviews the **data dashboard for the adaptive software** as well as marking other work. This informs future planning as well as the marking providing formative feedback for students *(It is important to highlight misconceptions)*.

Let's now consider how the same digital technology might be used within a Social Constructivist pedagogical stance.

Step 3: Aba's use of digital technology (social constructivist stance)

Remember to highlight aspects of this description that mirror how digital technology is used in your practice.

Aba's classroom has groups of tables with five or six learners per table. Learners are in mixed ability groups *(Pedagogical Belief: Where interaction is with someone who knows more about the subject than the learner does, the learner can achieve more than they would be able to achieve on their own).* Aba's class has access to a set of **mobile devices** (e.g. laptops, tablets), sufficient for the whole class working in pairs *(Teaching involves engaging learners in collaboration with others – through reconciling their different mental models, learning occurs).* Whilst Aba often plans who will be using the mobile devices, learners can ask to use them if they have a good reason for doing so *(Learners are active co-constructors of their knowledge).*

Prior to the lesson, Aba may have created **video clips** on how to carry out a particular procedure or an explanation of some specific information. Aba does this in order to encourage learners' independence during the lesson *(The role of the teacher is to scaffold learning).*

Aba uses a range of **accessibility features** to ensure a fully inclusive classroom. These include automated subtitles when using presentations, audio and video clips as stimuli, and presentation content that takes account of visual impairment and cognitive load *(The role of the teacher is to scaffold learning).* Learners in Aba's class utilise a range of **accessibility features** as and when the teacher or someone working with them (including other learners) suggests they may find them helpful. These include screen masks, talk-to-text, picture dictionaries, audio recording, voice-activated apps, zoom/screen magnification, and others.

Aba typically starts a session by projecting a stimulus onto a **large digital display** using a **visualiser** or a **laptop** which may be located anywhere in the classroom *(Teachers are seen as knowledgeable about different subject domains and how to direct learning; The role of the teacher is to scaffold learning).* The input might include **interactive images, film or audio clips, web pages, or augmented reality apps** to introduce key concepts and ideas and support learners in making connections *(Learners are co-constructors of their knowledge).* Aba regularly asks open questions and directs discussions about the topic *(Learning is reliant upon dialogue to co-construct understanding, which becomes part of the individuals' existing mental models).* Aba may use **interactive question-and-answer software** to gauge the learners' understanding of the topic. Once Aba feels that the majority of the class has understood the main points, groups of learners are directed to carry out activities related to the topic.

One group, working in pairs *(Teaching involves engaging learners in collaboration with others – through reconciling their different mental models, learning occurs),* might use **adaptive software that takes them through a series of questions** linked to the current topic, which automatically provides new questions or tasks based on correct answers to the previous question *(The purpose of education is to help learners develop organised, abstract mental models of the world, and procedures for applying them which are transferable across situations).*

Another group may use the **internet to search for information** within parameters set out by the teacher. Aba will normally direct the learners to specific websites or pages *(The role of the teacher is to scaffold learning).* The group's 'findings' might be recorded diagrammatically (e.g. as a **concept map**) which will then be handed in. Aba will then assess the extent to which the learners' understanding aligns with the accepted view within the subject domain *(Learners need to understand the nature of subject domains and the ways in which their knowledge bases are socially* *constructed).* Aba encourages learners to record their workings or thinking in an exercise book – which may be digital – as part of capturing ideas or strategies from their peers that can be used in future tasks.

Aba may set groups a task which requires learners to produce a **digital outcome** such as a set of **slides, an animation, a video, a document**, and so on. Learners may work in pairs or small groups to produce the digital outcome and are actively encouraged and taught to talk with each other about their ideas – extending each other's contributions and building new knowledge together *(Learning is reliant on dialogue to co-construct understanding, which becomes part of the individuals' existing mental models).* Where work is shared via **social media** the audience may acknowledge the work (e.g. 'likes', short comments, or some kind of recognition), but this will not usually include two-way interaction. Having a 'real' audience is seen as making the work meaningful *(learners want to make sense of how others in society see the world)*, but interaction with that audience is not normally encouraged. During the task, Aba asks open questions and supports learners in talking with each other productively *(The role of the teacher is to scaffold learning)*. As the task progresses Aba will share what different groups are doing with the rest of the class via the large **display** to stimulate further discussion *(Learners want to make sense of how others in society see the world).*

At the end of a session, Aba may use **quiz** software to ascertain the learners' understanding and reinforce key points *(Teachers are seen as knowledgeable about different subject domains and how to direct learning).* The learners work in teams and have time to talk prior to responding to each question. After each question, the correct answer is displayed, and Aba leads a discussion about why the answer is correct. Whilst the software may show which group has answered the most questions correctly Aba's focus is on using the software to clarify thinking and understand what aspects of the topic need additional input. Occasionally, Aba will get a group to create quiz questions, which will then be used with the whole class *(Learners are active co-constructors of their knowledge).*

The learners know that towards the end of the session, one of the groups will be asked to share their work with the rest of the class (*Learning is reliant on dialogue to co-construct understanding, which becomes part of the individuals' existing mental models*). They will do this by using, or projecting onto, the **large display**.

After the session, Aba reviews the **data dashboard in adaptive software** to inform interventions for groups of learners. Aba also marks completed work in order to give the learners constructive critical feedback *(The role of the teacher is to scaffold learning).*

Finally, let's consider how the same digital technology might be used within a Sociocultural Pedagogical Stance.

Step 4: Jo's use of digital technology (sociocultural stance)

Remember to highlight aspects of this description that mirror how digital technology is used in your practice.

Jo's **classroom** is set up so that it can be re-organised to suit the activities that are taking place. The approach is generally problem-based. Individual learners may be focused on different problems that are of particular interest to them personally *(Pedagogical Belief: Motivation is intrinsic – learners want to belong to particular communities and be recognised as valued members of them)*. These are often linked to their local community. Investigating a problem and deciding how to address it might take weeks to complete and involve inter-disciplinary work *(The purpose of education is to support learners in becoming competent in valued social practices, within a range of different communities)*. Learners are expected to work individually or in self-selected teams and can choose how they are going to approach their problem *(Learners are seen as active and agentive. They have multiple identities and competencies, each linked to the different communities they belong to)*. Each learner in Jo's class has their own **mobile device** (e.g. laptops, tablets), which they can use as and when they feel it is appropriate.

Jo and the learners each use a range of **accessibility features** – thinking about how best they each communicate with each other and how best to ensure inclusivity for others. These include automated subtitles when using presentations, audio and video feedback, audio and video clips to complement text, and presentation content that takes account of visual impairment and cognitive load *(The purpose of education is to support learners in becoming competent in valued social practices)*.

At the start of each day, Jo leads a whole-class session to sort out organisational issues and hear from individuals and teams about how their work is progressing and to discuss any issues that they need help with *(The role of the teacher is to orchestrate support available to learners)*. Jo encourages learners to talk to each other about the full range of ideas in that shared space – exploring themes and patterns and posing their own consequent questions. This may involve learners sharing what they are working on (e.g. digital documents, forum discussions) using a large **digital display**. Jo asks open questions and encourages learners to capture their ideas on their mobile devices, review contributions by others, and extend or build on each other's ideas.

Following the whole-class discussion at the start of the day, individuals and teams then carry on with their work. Jo works alongside learners, sometimes providing direct instruction, sometimes modelling how to approach a task, sometimes learning in conjunction with them *(Teaching involves connecting classroom activities to valued practices in the world and making meanings explicit for learners to use)*.

The **Internet** is a critical tool for Jo's learners as it enables them to find information and engage with communities beyond the school *(The purpose of education is to support learners in becoming competent in valued social practices, within a range of different communities, each of which has its own shared objectives and valued ways of working)*. Given the different foci of their work, Jo expects learners to search the Internet to find relevant information. Learners may use **concept maps** to help them organise and make sense of information. They use **digital documents** of various sorts (e.g. **slides, podcasts, video and audio clips, animations**, etc.) to record and share their work. They communicate with people beyond the school using a range of tools including **social media (e.g. blogs), discussion forums,**

email, and videoconferencing *(Learning involves mutually agreeing on meaning through interaction).*

How the learners work, the tools and competencies that they use, and the outcomes that they aim to achieve reflect the issue or problem that they are addressing in the context of the community involved. Part of Jo's role is to help the learners understand how different communities operate and what are seen as appropriate and valued ways of working within those communities *(Teaching involves connecting classroom activities to valued practices in the world and making meanings explicit for learners to use).* Often, Jo is learning from or alongside the learners.

Learners know that their problem-based projects will culminate in a **presentation** that aims to summarise what they have learnt. These presentations will be shared with a range of audiences beyond the school. The intention is that their work will have an impact – this might be in highlighting an issue or stimulating action to address it or some other tangible outcome *(Knowledge is the ability to act in meaningful ways within particular communities, which have shared goals and shared valued ways of working).* Their presentations will generally include a **range of media (e.g. video, audio, animations, text, images**, etc.), much of which they will have created themselves. Occasionally, the learners will use **quiz software** to create sets of questions which will act as a provocation – to encourage others to think about the issue and how it might be addressed.

Step 5: Reflecting on your own practice

As you read through the preceding examples in Steps 1–4, you will have recognised some or many Pedagogical Practices and will have highlighted aspects of the practice that mirrored things you do in your practice.

Look back through the four exemplars, and then circle **one** pedagogical stance that your highlighting suggests that your Pedagogical Practices most closely align with.

My current Pedagogical Practice when using digital technology most closely aligns with:			
Traditional	Individual Constructivist	Social Constructivist	Sociocultural

If you have highlighted extracts from more than one of the preceding exemplars, it suggests a misalignment within your practice. You may want to think more about how to ensure greater consistency in your practice – we explore this further in Chapter 8.

To support your reflection, Table 7.2 provides a short summary of how each of the different digital technology examples from earlier have been used by the teacher personas with different Pedagogical Stances.

Table 7.2 Summary of how digital technology is used differently by different teacher personas

	Niq (Traditional)	**Sam (Individual constructivist)**	**Aba (Social constructivist)**	**Jo (Sociocultural)**
Mobile devices (e.g. laptops, tablets)	Class set (sufficient for one each). Use planned by teacher	Class set (sufficient for one each). Use planned by teacher, but learners can ask to use them	Sufficient for one between two (does not want one-to-one). Use planned by teacher, but learners can ask to use them	Each learner has a device, which they consider to be their own. Learners choose when and how to use their devices
Assistive technology	Specific accessibility adaptations for those with identified special needs	Used by pre-identified learners when perceived as useful	Used when perceived to be useful (by the teacher or learner)	Used when perceived to be useful (by the teacher or learner)
Large display + presentation software	Teacher presentation, with closed questions	Teacher presentation with open and closed question	Teacher presentation with open questions, directs discussion To share what groups are doing with the rest of the class	Learners may share their work during whole class sessions or when giving presentations (e.g. at the end of a project)
Images/Video/ Audio clips	Used in teacher presentations to engage the learners. Video for those who complete other work early	Teacher-created video clips to explain information and/or procedures. Used in teacher presentations to encourage focused discussion. May be learner-created (individual contributions clearly identifiable)	Teacher-created video clips to explain information and/or procedures. Used in teacher presentations to introduce/explain key concepts and ideas. May be learner created (collaboratively – one per group)	Sourced or created by learners

(Continued)

Table 7.2 (Continued)

	Niq (Traditional)	**Sam (Individual constructivist)**	**Aba (Social constructivist)**	**Jo (Sociocultural)**
Question-and-answer software (Displays question and all the learners' answers)		Whole class or group Anonymised answers	Whole class or group	
Quiz software	Respond individually No discussion of answers or between questions Music and timer to increase pace Leaderboard to enhance competition	Respond individually Teacher-led discussion of answers after each question (to address misconceptions) Focus on clarifying thinking rather than competition	Respond in teams Discussion within the team before answering each question Discussion of answers after each question Focus on clarifying thinking rather than competition Groups may create quizzes for other learners	May be used by learners to create provocations
Drill-and-practice software (Asks questions, shows whether right or wrong)	Lower ability learners, individually Shows score			
Adaptive software (Presents information, route through material decided by responses learner gives to questions)	Middle-ability learners Shows progress and performance relative to others	Work individually Teacher reviews incorrect answers with learners to surface misconceptions	Work in pairs (collaborative) Teacher reviews incorrect answers with learners to surface misconceptions	

(*Continued*)

	Niq (Traditional)	Sam (Individual constructivist)	Aba (Social constructivist)	Jo (Sociocultural)
The web	High-ability learners Pre-selected websites Individually answering questions set by teacher	Use specific websites Individually or in pairs (cooperative – recording individually)	Search within teacher-set parameters Work as a group (collaborative)	Critical tool 'Free search' by learners
Concept maps		Created individually	Created collaboratively (one per group)	Created individually or collaboratively
Cloud-based editable documents (e.g. documents, slides, spreadsheets, websites)		In pairs or small groups Task divided up so each has 'their own' section to complete	In collaborative pairs or small groups – individual contributions not identifiable	May be used to collaborate with others within or beyond the school
Social media (e.g. class blog, Twitter, discussion forums)	Teacher selects examples of 'best work' to post Comments not enabled	To share work via class blog Third parties leave comments, moderated by teacher	To share work via class blog Third parties leave comments Two-way communication not encouraged (for 'child protection' reasons)	Discuss/collaborate with others beyond the school Share work – aiming to have an impact beyond school

Step 6: Mapping enacted practice to conscious pedagogical beliefs

We can now consider the alignment between our Conscious Pedagogical Beliefs (identified back in Chapter 4), and our Enacted Practice when using digital technology (from this Guided Activity). Return to the activities indicated in the following box, and circle which pedagogical stance each aligned with.

In Activity **4.2**, Step 6 my **Conscious Pedagogical Beliefs** aligned with:	Traditional Individual Constructivist Social Constructivist Sociocultural
In Activity **7.2**, Step 5 my **Enacted** practice when using **digital technology** aligned with:	Traditional Individual Constructivist Social Constructivist Sociocultural
Did your conscious Pedagogical Beliefs (from Activity 4.2 Step 6) align with the pedagogical stance underpinning your enacted Pedagogical Practice with digital technology (from Activity 7.2 Step 5)?	Yes / No
How did comparing these alignments make you feel? What did this process prompt you to think about?	

At this point, don't be alarmed if the Pedagogical Stance evident in your Conscious Beliefs and underpinning your Enacted Practice did not align – that is not unusual! In the next chapter, we look at 'Closing the Pedagogical Alignment Gap'.

Impact by design

A key issue when using digital technology in your teaching is the impact that you want it to have. The Digital Technology Impact Framework (DTIF) suggests that when you are learning WITH digital technology, as opposed to learning ABOUT it or OTHER, then there are three categories of impact that might be achieved (see Figure 7.2).

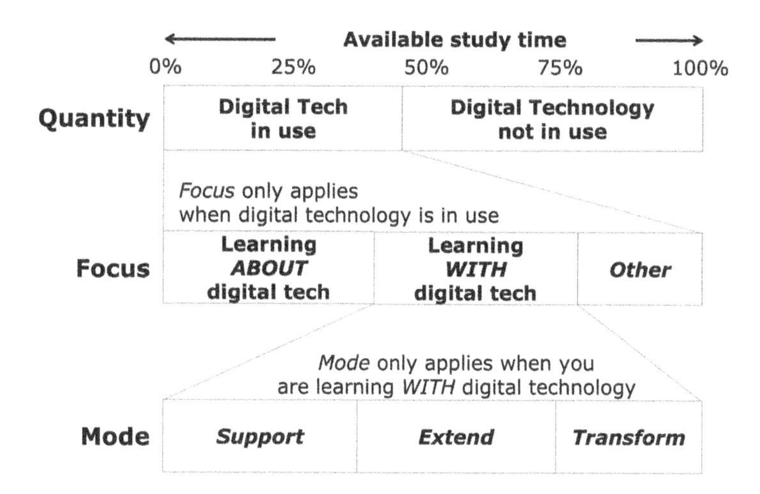

Figure 7.2 Diagrammatic overview of the digital technology impact framework (DTIF) showing the mode or impact dimension

The three categories of Mode (degrees of impact) are defined in relation to changes in what is being learnt and/or how it is being learnt, as illustrated in Figure 7.3.

The DTIF does not intend to suggest that any one Mode is better than the others. This depends on what you value – your Pedagogical Stance. Evidence from the NP3 project (Twining et al., 2017) suggests that as time spent learning WITH digital technology increases, there is a corresponding shift in the Mode dimension

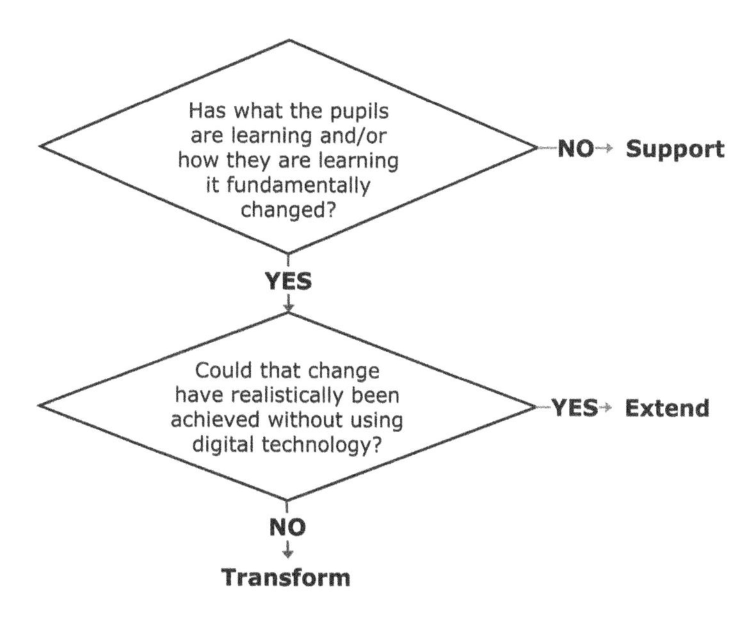

Figure 7.3 Flowchart for defining categories on the mode dimension

from Support to Extend and Transform. However, this does not appear to be a causal relationship; increasing the time spent using digital technology does not appear to change the pedagogical stance (Maher & Twining, 2016). Rather, where a teacher has been limited in fully implementing their Pedagogical Beliefs, using digital technology can turbo boost their practice:

> The way I approach my teaching hasn't changed. But it's the tools that I've got at my fingertips that have really changed. That said though, in the past, before having all these devices I hadn't felt as though we can go as far as I wanted to go with that sort of process. I mean it's a constructivist approach [Yeah]. That's never changed for me but I can do it to a greater, it's constructivism on steroids.
>
> *(Primary school teacher interview, quoted in Maher & Twining, 2016, p. 86)*

The three categories on the Mode dimension seem to align with the different Pedagogical Stances:

- Support with Traditional
- Extend with Individual Constructivist
- Transform with Social Constructivist and Sociocultural

Whilst much of the rhetoric about digital technology in education is about transformation, if your pedagogical stance is Traditional, then you are likely to be better served by using digital technology to Support rather than Extend or Transform your practice.

Conclusion

We must all remember that we must not use any kind of digital technology (or indeed any kind of resource or tool) unless we have a clear understanding of how it will enhance the learning in our classroom. Alongside this, we must make sure that any resource use aligns with (and supports) our Pedagogical Beliefs. This is what will create effective pedagogy.

Note

1 The DTIF is fundamentally the same as the ICT Innovation Framework (ICTIF) that was used by the NP3 Project (https://edfutures.net/NP3) – the only differences being the labels used in the Quantity and Focus dimensions.

References

Aldosemani, T. (2019) "Inservice Teachers' Perceptions of a Professional Development Plan Based on SAMR Model: A Case Study', *The Turkish Online Journal of Educational Technology*, 18(3), pp. 46–53.

Cherner, T., and Mitchell, C. (2021) 'Deconstructing EdTech Frameworks based on Their Creators, Features, and Usefulness', *Learning, Media and Technology*, 46(1), pp. 91–116.

Christodoulou, D. (2020) *Teachers vs Tech?: The Case for An Ed Tech Revolution*. Oxford: Oxford University Press.

Dwyer, D. C., Ringstaff, C., and Sandholtz, J. H. (1990). *Teacher Beliefs and Practices Part I: Patterns of Change. The Evolution of Teachers Instructional Beliefs and Practices in High-Access-To-Technology Classrooms. First to Fourth Year Findings*. Cupertino: Apple Computer.

EdTech Evidence Exchange (2021) U.S. K-12 Public Education Technology Spending. https://edtechevidence.org/report/U-S-K-12-Public-Education-Technology-Spending/

Education Endowment Foundation (2019) Digital Technology to Improve Learning: An Evidence Review. London.

Education Select Committee (2022) *The Impact of COVID-19 on Education and Children's Services*. London: Education Select Committee.

Higgins, S., Xiao, Z., and Katsipataki, M. (2012) The Impact of Digital Technology on Learning: A Summary for the Education Endowment Foundation Full Report. London.

IMARC (2022) *Digital Classroom Market: Global Industry Trends, Share, Size, Growth, Opportunity and Forecast 2022–2027*. New York: IMARC.

Maher, D., and Twining, P. (2016) 'Bring Your Own Device–A Snapshot of Two Australian Primary Schools', *Educational Research*, 59(1), pp. 73–88.

Mishra, P., and Koehler, M. J. (2006) 'Technological Pedagogical Content Knowledge (TPACK) Framework – Educational Technology', *Teachers College Record*, 108(6), pp. 1017–1054.

Moane, F. (2019) 'Interweaving Traditional and Digital Approaches', *Impact: The Journal of the Chartered College of Teaching* (2019 Special Edition: Education Technology, January 2019).

Naace (2018) *Naace: The Naace Self Review Framework*. Southampton: NAACE.

Organisation for Economic Co-ordination and Development (2022) *Education Policy Outlook 2022: Transforming Pathways for Lifelong Learners*. London: OECD.

Oxford University Press (2022) *Addressing the Deepening Digital Divide*. London: OUP.

Puentedura, R. (2010) *SAMR and TPCK: Intro to Advanced Practice*.

Twining, P. (2008) 'Framing IT Use to Enhance Educational Impact on a School-wide basis', in Voogt, J., and Knezek, G. (eds.) *International Handbook of Information Technology in Primary and Secondary Education*. New York: Springer, pp. 555–577.

Twining, P. (2018) *The Digital Technology Impact Framework (DTIF)*. The half-baked.education blog. November 30th 2018. https://halfbaked.education/the-digital-practice-framework/

Twining et al. (2017) NP3 New Purposes, New Practices, New Pedagogy: Meta-analysis Report. The Society for Educational Studies.

UNESCO (2021) *Reimagining Our Futures Together: A New Social Contract for Education*. Paris: UNESCO.

CHAPTER

8

Closing the pedagogical alignment gap

The last seven chapters have focused heavily on the importance of making your own Pedagogical Beliefs explicit. We have encouraged you to think about the extent to which your Pedagogical Beliefs are aligned with your Pedagogical Intentions and your Pedagogical Practices when using digital technology.

Alignment between Pedagogical Beliefs, Intentions, and Practices is important because it brings consistency to what is experienced by our learners. Ultimately, if we are part of the teaching profession in order to support learning, it is what is experienced and internalised by our learners that matters the most. It is vitally important that we remember that the learners' experiences and their internalisations are what make a difference to their learning.

When our Pedagogical Beliefs, Intentions, and Practices are not in alignment, we send confused messages to our learners about what it means to be a learner and to learn, what it means to be a teacher and to teach, what knowledge is and how it is formed, and the goals of schooling. It is highly likely that you will have practical experience of witnessing confused messages in everyday life – where a person's literal words say one thing but their facial expression, body language, tone of voice, prioritisation, or practical actions suggest something different.

There are a number of potential ways in which different aspects of your pedagogy may be misaligned; there may be alignment gaps between:

- your **Conscious Beliefs** (I believe that … which aligns with a … stance) and your **Pedagogical Intentions** (I am going to … which suggests I believe that … which aligns with a … stance)
- your **Pedagogical Intentions** (I am going to … which suggests I believe that … which aligns with a … stance) and
  your **Pedagogical Practices** (What I did was … which suggests I believe that … which aligns with a … stance)

DOI: 10.4324/9781003321637-8

- Your **Conscious Beliefs** (I believe that … which aligns with a … stance) and your **Pedagogical Practices** (What I did was … which suggests I believe that … which aligns with a … stance)

Everyday examples of this include the following:

Example 1

I believe that …	learners are intrinsically motivated	which aligns with a **Constructivist or Sociocultural stance**
I am going to …	set digitally timed activities and online leaderboards to encourage learners to work hard and/or behave in a particular way, which suggests I believe that motivation is extrinsic and enhanced by competition	which aligns with a **Traditional stance**

Example 2

I am going to …	ensure learners are extending each other's ideas as they collaborate on a joint task as a powerful part of supporting their learning, which suggests I believe that dialogue is essential as it enables co-construction of knowledge	which aligns with a **Social Constructivist stance**
What I did was …	encourage learners to talk to each other about their work whilst they complete their individual version of the task, which suggests I believe that learning is an individual activity, but dialogue may be potentially useful if it creates cognitive conflict that enables individuals to adapt their own mental models	which aligns with an **Individual Constructivist** stance

Example 3

I believe that …	knowledge is 'out there' ready to be acquired by learners	which aligns with a **Traditional** stance
What I did was …	get learners to compare how 'the same' words are used in different contexts to mean different things, which suggests I believe that meaning is socially defined and depends on the context	which aligns with a **Social Constructivist or Sociocultural** stance

Whilst your Intended Practice is likely to be underpinned by your Conscious Beliefs, you may have discovered some misalignment between the Pedagogical Stance underpinning your Intended and your Enacted Practice (in Activity 6.3) and/or your Conscious Beliefs and those underpinning your Enacted Practice (Activity 7.2). Both these things point to a lack of alignment with your implicit beliefs, because your Enacted Practice is likely to reflect your Implicit Beliefs because we live out what feels instinctive to us (Hamachek, 1999). In this chapter, our focus is on bringing greater alignment between these components (Conscious Beliefs, Enacted Practice, and Implicit Beliefs). We refer to this process as *Closing the Pedagogical Alignment Gap.*

Defining a pedagogical alignment gap

It is important to remember that this book has been focusing on you as an individual human being – drawing out the personal and professional influences which shape your thinking and actions about using digital technology to support learning. Yet you (as an individual) will be working within a particular school (context). Therefore, there will be three sets of pedagogical alignment that are important to consider:

- Your **personal** Pedagogical Alignment Gap – addressing any misalignment between your Pedagogical Beliefs, Intentions, and Practices
- Your **organisational-based** Pedagogical Alignment Gap, which has two elements:
  - addressing any misalignment between your personal Pedagogical Beliefs, Intentions and Practices, and those relating to the context that you work within (e.g. your school)
  - addressing any misalignment within the school (e.g. between different school policies or norms)

It is unlikely that any of us will achieve perfect alignment between our Pedagogical Beliefs, Intentions and Practice 100% of the time. Similarly, it is unlikely for there to be perfect alignment between every teacher within a school and any pedagogical stance promoted by the organisation. However, it is important that we all aim to reduce the gaps in order that we all benefit from clear and consistent messages about our role in supporting learning. This helps us work together more effectively – underpinning and promoting collective efficacy (Hoogsteen, 2020; Hattie, 2018).

Addressing a personal pedagogical alignment gap

When we think about closing our personal Pedagogical Alignment Gap, we have five choices:

1) Change our Pedagogical Beliefs
2) Change our Pedagogical Intentions
3) Change our Pedagogical Practices
4) A combination of the above
5) Accept misalignment and the consequent impact on our learners

By not addressing our pedagogical alignment, by default we defer to the last of those options (Choice 5), and our pedagogy will be less effective. If our professional purpose is to support learning as effectively as possible, there is an ethical friction created by accepting misalignment and not attempting to reduce the Pedagogical Alignment Gap.

In practice your Conscious Beliefs and Intended Practice are likely to be aligned because they are both visible to you – you are conscious of what both are. The major challenge is in identifying gaps between your Conscious Beliefs, your Implicit Beliefs and your Enacted Practice.

In Activity 6.3, you will have identified the extent of alignment between the beliefs underpinning your Intended Practice (i.e. your Conscious Beliefs) and Enacted Practice (i.e. your Implicit Beliefs). In Activity 7.2, you will have identified the extent of alignment between your Conscious Beliefs and the beliefs underpinning your Enacted Practice. In both these cases, a mismatch suggests one of two things:

1) Your Conscious Beliefs and your Implicit Beliefs may not be the same. In other words, you don't actually believe what you think you believe.
2) There are influences which are preventing you from enacting your Conscious Beliefs.

In order to close your Pedagogical Alignment Gap, you may wish to do the following:

- Invest time in making your Implicit Beliefs explicit and thus reconcile a gap between your previously Implicit and Conscious Beliefs – addressing Option 1 earlier (revisit Chapter 6).
- Identify the influences which are preventing you from Enacting your Conscious Beliefs – addressing Option 2 above – see the section which follows on closing an organisational alignment gap

Changing our pedagogical practice

A great deal has been written about how (as teachers) we might change our teaching practice (e.g. Lemov, 2021, Sims et al., 2021; Sharples, 2019; Fletcher-Wood, 2018; Fullan et al., 2018; Cordingley et al., 2015; Timperley et al., 2007). We do not intend to replicate the work of school leaders and academics by repeating those findings here. However, we do encourage you to revisit the ideas that you may have read or heard about previously, utilising the guidance in Chapter 2. You now have a deeper understanding of your own Pedagogical Beliefs and your personal Funnels of Influence, which will affect how you translate ideas into practice.

Similarly, a great deal has also been written about how we can more effectively support learning – although (as discussed in Chapter 2), largely with a focus on replicable processes and measurable outcomes (e.g. Willingham, 2021; Hattie & Smith, 2022; Sherrington & Caviglioli, 2020; Burns & Griffith, 2018; William, 2017; Hattie, 2014). We encourage you to revisit teaching strategies that you are already familiar with from your reading and discussions and consider – with your now deeper understanding of your own Pedagogical Beliefs – the influences that affect you personally and impact how you consequently implement these ideas.

As a teacher, you probably have more agency than you think (Twining & Aubrey-Smith, 2021; Priestley et al., 2015). Sometimes, in schools we are more aware of the limitations that we work within than the Opportunities that are available to us. In Chapter 5, when we introduced the Funnels of Influence, we set out how the Situational Self interprets the contextual Opportunities – and we each then see a sub-set as Possibilities that are available to us. The choices that we see as available to us depend on how we see ourselves (our identity) in that context in that Moment of Practice. We may (or may not) be able to change the context, but we can change how we conceptualise ourselves in that moment (e.g. Bandler, 2013).

Let's briefly unpack an example.

Imagine that your school has subscribed to quiz software and requires you to use it. At the surface level, this suggests that your Practice becomes defined by your context. However, you could do the following:

- Use the quiz software to provide individual summative assessments at the end of tasks or lessons (Traditional)
- Use the quiz software to provide formative assessments at key points in the lesson – identifying misconceptions (Individual Constructivist)
- Use the quiz software for learners to complete quizzes in pairs or teams – discussing which answers may be right or wrong and why (Social Constructivist)
- Having your learners create quizzes that will act as provocations for other people in order to highlight an issue or stimulate debate (Sociocultural)

In each case, you are using the quiz software that the school has subscribed to, but *how* and *why* it is being incorporated into classroom practice vary considerably, reflecting different Pedagogical Stances – and underlying Pedagogical Beliefs about teaching, learning, and knowledge.

Many teachers wait for direction (often perceived as permission) from their headteacher/principal before trying out new ideas, assuming (often incorrectly) that their headteacher/principal has the time and motivation to absorb the detail.

But as teachers, we need to be more open to the idea that our leaders usually trust and empower us more than we think – as long as we focus on making a positive impact on enhancing learning.

In today's political educational climate, we often hear colleagues talking about the increased global focus on assessment and comparative data (Salhberg, 2015). This results in a perception that there are limitations about what can consequently take place in the classroom. This is true – but perhaps not as much as it at first appears. There are still a lot of choices available to us all as teachers – if we think carefully about our Pedagogical Beliefs (what we are trying to achieve through our role as teacher and why) and take a conscious decision to act, with increasing precision, in order to translate those beliefs into aligned Pedagogical Practices, for example, how we act on learner questions or responses, how much we choose to trust our learners, and how we help learners connect their ideas in school with their wider lives beyond (and vice versa).

If we want to make meaningful changes to our **Practice**, we need to first become explicitly aware of what we believe practice should look like. Importantly, what we personally believe practice should look like, not just an adopted view that has been espoused by others.

Part of understanding whether we want to change our Beliefs or our Practice is about understanding what is influencing the way that these emerge from within us. In Chapter 5, we introduced The Funnels of Influence – a model which unpacks influences from both the context we are in at any given moment (The Context Funnel) and influences that are coming from within us (The Self Funnel). Unpacking those influences helps us be clearer about why we believe, say, and do the things that we do and where the catalysts or barriers to refining or changing those may be located.

It is useful to consider whether the changes that we want (or need) to make to our beliefs or practices are underpinned by influences from 'The Self' or from 'The Context'. It is important to note that most influences and changes will be a mix of both, but identifying the predominant underpinning influences will help us understand exactly where to focus our energy when making changes. In other words, if a contextual influence is affecting what we think and do, then to what extent will that contextual influence also affect future practice, and to what extent can we change that influence? Or, if it is our 'Self' that is affecting what we think and do, then to what extent will that 'Self' also affect future practice, and to what extent can we change our 'Self'? Once we know what the catalysts or barriers are, then clarity about our next steps is more likely to emerge.

Guided Activity 8.1: Closing a pedagogical alignment gap

Purpose: To be clear about practical next steps for closing a personal Pedagogical Alignment Gap.

Time needed: 15 minutes

We strongly recommend you use the editable version of this Guided Activity, which you can download from www.onelifelearning.co.uk/resources

In the following table, identify what your tangible next steps will be to closing your personal Pedagogical Alignment Gap.

What does my Enacted Practice suggest about my **Implicit Beliefs,** and how might I go about unpacking or exploring them?	
Do I need to change my **Conscious Beliefs**? If so, what will I do, how and when?	
Do I need to change my **Pedagogical Practices**? If so, which aspects of the Funnels of Influence do I need to spend more time exploring? (See Chapter 5.)	
Or will I accept misalignment and the consequent impact on my learners? If so, what might that impact be?	

From individual alignment to organisational alignment

Previously, we set out that there may be a context-based Pedagogical Alignment Gap: a gap between an organisation's implicit or espoused ('conscious') beliefs, pedagogical expectations (Intentions), and/or Enacted Practices (TPEA, 2022). For example, a Teaching and Learning policy may specify particular practices that teachers are expected to implement (Intentions), which are underpinned by Pedagogical Beliefs that may be overt or implicit. Clearly, there are many potential permutations where misalignment is possible.

Thus far, this chapter has focused on closing your individual Pedagogical Alignment Gap. However, what happens if there is a misalignment between your individual Pedagogical Beliefs and the Pedagogical Beliefs that are embedded within your school, or there are inconsistencies in the Pedagogical Stance underpinning school policies and norms?

First, it is important to be clear about what we mean by your school in this context. A school in itself does not have a voice to be able to espouse Pedagogical Beliefs. Pedagogical Beliefs are instead espoused by either

- an individual leader with an expectation that others will adopt the beliefs or
- by a group of people (e.g. senior leadership team, or perhaps even a majority of the school staff), with an assumption that the beliefs are shared to a greater or lesser degree. Examples of this might include policy documents or expectations of practice ('at our school we all aim to …').

The perception of alignment with the organisationally espoused Pedagogical Beliefs will probably depend on how involved the person speaking or listening was with the process of agreeing them. In other words, those who lead or participate meaningfully in setting a school vision and strategy (which usually assumes a particular set of Pedagogical Beliefs) are more likely to be aligned with it. Those who did not participate in its creation may identify less with its implied or overt (Conscious) Pedagogical Stance (Fullan, 2020; Hargreaves, 2018).

Considering this challenge pragmatically, there are some simple questions that we can each ask ourselves, focusing attention on the Context aspect of the Funnels of Influence (Chapter 5), for example, 'What is possible for us to change in our context?' Specifically probing the following:

1) Situational Features (What could I change in this moment of practice?)
2) Classroom Arena (What stable features of my classroom can I change?)
3) School Arena (What stable aspects of the school can I influence?)
4) Broader Context (What stable aspects beyond my school should I bring to the attention of my colleagues so that we can respond to them collectively?)

Talking consciously about Pedagogical Beliefs with colleagues is important (Hargreaves, 2000). However, as we have explored, you need to be aware that what people espouse may not be what they implicitly believe.

We usually think about what we want to say or write before we communicate. This allows us to consciously focus on how we communicate – we 'frame' what we want to say (Nelson et al., 1997). In addition, the environment around us gently encourages some forms of change. For example, when we hear phrases regularly, we tend to subconsciously or consciously repeat them (Bernstein, 1971). As professionals, we adopt terminology, phrases, and views on debates from colleagues, leaders, the media, and the wider sector – which we then find ourselves incorporating into our own forms of communication (Wilson, 1990). We might do this intentionally (e.g. to reflect our understanding or knowledge or to align ourselves with a particular group of people by using shared vocabulary). Or we might do it unintentionally (e.g. we hear a phrase or word so often that we just end up repeating it out of habit rather than necessarily understanding it or agreeing with it).

As you may be aware, there is an abundance of meaning layered into our language. Yet discourse analysis (the process of unpacking that meaning) is rarely used within general education research and rarer still in research concerned with digital technology in education (Tannen et al., 2015).

There are two particular aspects of discourse analysis that are useful to be aware of when considering how teachers and learners interact with digital technology. First, when we talk about something we 'frame' the conversation by fore-fronting particular aspects and giving less attention to (or excluding) other aspects. For example, this book frames the conversation about digital technology around pedagogy – we are not addressing other aspects of digital technology such as infrastructure or eSafety. This idea of 'Framing' emerges from Centering Theory (Walker et al., 1998). In conversation, teachers may frame ideas about digital technology consciously because of a particular motivation or agenda or subconsciously due to levels of knowledge or confidence in the subject matter or the relationship with their audience. It's important to be aware that there are usually many more threads to a conversation than the ones we choose to feature. Through our choices, we are in effect filtering for our audience (which can be either helpful or unhelpful).

Furthermore, when we interact with others, meaning accumulates over the course of that interaction. In a conversation, the nature of the interactions at the beginning determines the consequent flow between those involved, setting parameters and conveying intentions. Phrases used later in the conversation will often refer back to aspects covered earlier or will assume shared understanding based on what has already been discussed. These features are known as dialogic undertones, which are an important aspect of human interaction that is also often not considered (Hodges, 2015). Dialogic undertones shape how we understand what is being said in light of past shared experiences or dialogue. Therefore, if we want to make changes to what we espouse, we need to reflect on these features, the messages that they are conveying, and why we may be consciously or subconsciously doing so. By making these implicit messages explicit, we are then able to address and refine our future espousals.

As well as reflecting on these ideas yourself, encourage colleagues to become more aware about

- the influence of individual Pedagogical Beliefs on everyday practice (revisit Chapters 4 and 7 which illustrate this through practical examples)
- the importance of making individual Pedagogical Beliefs explicit – and how to identify what those beliefs are (revisit Chapters 4, 6, and 7)
- the huge range of influences which shape every single Moment of Practice (revisit the Funnels of Influence in Chapter 5)
- the importance of closing Pedagogical Alignment Gaps (to enhance our pedagogical effectiveness).

The single greatest influence that you can have on closing the Pedagogical Alignment Gaps across your school is to actively encourage your colleagues to talk regularly, explicitly, and precisely about Pedagogical Practices and Beliefs. This form of discourse promotes self and collective awareness about how those beliefs relate to everyday practice, and – most important – the impact that our Pedagogical Beliefs have on our learners.

Whilst any one of us can engage colleagues in pedagogical discussion, we may not all be in a position to do so formally. If you have a leadership role or the opportunity to influence professional learning provision in your school, you might implement the following team development activities.

Team development activities

These activities will help you to lead colleagues to identify and then close the Pedagogical Alignment Gaps that are probably present in your school.

Ideally, these activities will involve all those involved in decision-making and classroom practice within your school or organisation. This should include those in leadership, teaching and learning roles (e.g. senior and middle leaders, teachers, support staff) as well as those supporting digital technology use (e.g. information technology [IT] leaders and operational colleagues). For groups of schools, this activity should also include the executive or central team.

The activities probe influences, intentions, and practices and, as such, will be dependent on at least some of those involved being able to reflect on pedagogy.

Some schools may prefer to carry out this activity as a leadership team. This can work effectively in surfacing key considerations and helping develop a strategy. However, the impact on classroom practice is dependent on the engagement of teaching and support staff.

You could do these activities on your own in order to develop a better understanding of your own school. However, that is likely to produce a biased view – each of us sees slightly different things in the world around us, and those differences all affect your school context.

These activities have been designed as a sequence of two separate activities that you can either spread over a series of weeks (e.g. one activity per week as part of existing staff meetings) or work through as part of professional learning time.

Each activity contains a task which aims to surface specific information which will stimulate thinking and professional discussions.

Activity A: Identifying the influences affecting how digital technology is used in your school
Activity B: Understanding your school's Pedagogical Beliefs

Team Development Activity A: The influences affecting digital technology at your school

Purpose: To identify the key influences affecting how digital technology is used to support learning in your school/organisation.

Suggested Approach: This activity is best carried out as an initial concept mapping session, followed by a more methodical review. This ensures that coverage and consideration have been given to the many potential influences. The facilitator will need to prompt colleagues to really probe their thinking throughout the activity.

- Step 1: Identify an Influence
- Step 2: Where does that influence come from?
- Step 3: Surfacing more influences and their sources
- Step 4: Using the Funnels of Influence
- Step 5: Review the influences

Time needed: Allow 40 minutes for Steps 1–4, followed by 20 minutes for Step 5.

We strongly recommend you use the editable version of this Guided Activity, which you can download from www.onelifelearning.co.uk/resources

Step 1: Identify an influence

Ask colleagues to write on a sticky note (or digital equivalent) **one thing that they feel influences current digital technology practice and direction** in your school.

You may wish to give colleagues some initial prompts to encourage thinking *(e.g. influences could include the equipment available, a particular teaching method, the vision, or support of leaders).*

Note: Later stages of this activity sequence recommend colour coding to help you see trends and patterns. Therefore, you will find it helpful if colleagues all use one colour of pen/sticky note for each step unless the activity instructions recommend otherwise.

Step 2: Where does that influence come from?

Ask colleagues to think about the influence they have just identified – and to then probe it more forensically – what created that influence?

For example,

- What determines which equipment is available? (e.g. how were products or features chosen?)
- Why is the school using that particular teaching method? (e.g. what was the trigger to its adoption?)
- What support is available? (e.g. who advises and supports, when, where, why and how?)

Ask colleagues to capture this second layer of influence by adding another sticky note to the bottom of the original one – creating a visual trail of where the influences are coming from.

Add each pair of sticky notes to a shared display where you can all see what others are adding as this will help you to prompt each other's thinking.

Step 3: Surfacing more influences and their sources

Invite colleagues to **repeat Steps 1 and 2**. This time, aim to dig even deeper into where the influences come from. Continue this process, building up ideas on the shared display.

You will need to prompt colleagues to think deeply about not only the influences but what created them.

Step 4: Using the funnels of influence

There will come a point when the group feels that the main influences have been captured. This usually happens when surface-level influences have been identified. This is when meaningful probing now begins.

At this point, you may find it helpful to use the structure from the Funnels of Influence (in Chapter 5) – specifically the Context Funnel – to prompt colleagues to surface aspects which have not yet been considered. At this stage, don't worry about the theory behind the Funnels of Influence – just use the ideas to help trigger conversation and thinking.

Capture these ideas by adding them to the sticky note display that you have been building up.

For example,

a) What are the **Broader Context** influences (e.g. global trends, national policy, economic landscape, media narratives, cultural expectations)?

b) What are influences within your **School Arena** (e.g. school vision and values, mission, policies, strategic objectives and direction, budget landscape, current staffing profile, expectations)? Who drives these influences and how does their role or character affect what they say and how others perceive those messages?
c) What influences are there on each person's **Classroom Arena** (e.g. digital technology available in that classroom, additional adults, age and needs of the learners, how the classroom is set up, what the classroom norms are)? Who drives these influences, and what difference do the people in that classroom make to how those influences impact on practice?

Step 5: Review the influences

As a group, review all the sticky notes together. Use the Funnels of Influence to help you do this. Write headings on the sticky note display for the Context Funnel:

- Broader Context
- School Arena
- Classroom Arena
- Situational Features
- If you are part of a network of schools, you could add a heading for influences across the network – the Network Arena.

As a team, group the sticky notes under the Funnels of Influence headings. What do you notice?

Notes:

- It is important to discuss together the range of influences – sharing observations about ones which you are all aware of and others which only some colleagues may be aware of. Are there any that some staff feel are stronger influences than others? You may wish to explore why that is the case – what is creating those perceptions?
- It is very unusual for people to identify any influences that come from the Self Funnel at this stage. Where people surface influences relating to people, these usually relate to people other than themselves, and usually people in specific roles such as school leaders and/or technical support roles. This is absolutely fine – keep the focus on the Context at this stage. However, if colleagues do draw out influences from the Self, encourage discussion to focus on whether those influences are catalysts for action or barriers preventing action.
- Sometimes people refer to the provision of training or support which will usually be an influence from the School Arena.
- It is important to keep in mind that each person involved in this conversation will perceive these influences slightly differently. This might include feelings of ownership (e.g. about strategies or policies) and feelings of responsibility (e.g. about buying or maintaining equipment) and may include feelings of pride, embarrassment, excitement, or fear depending on how each *individual* person

has responded to each influence. This is all normal. However, as an empathetic professional, you may wish to remind colleagues to keep a focus on the tangible organisational influences that are affecting students' experiences, *not* on individual people's behaviours and skills.

Outcome:

At the end of this task, you are aiming to have a visual display reflecting the many different influences that are currently shaping the practice and direction of digital technology use within your school. This display will reflect which influences are located within the classroom, school, and group/region (if relevant) and from the Broader Context.

This activity should give you a clear sense of the many (contextual) influences that are affecting current practice and direction when using digital technology. It should also provide a feel for which of those influences are the most important and who drives them.

What you now need to do is to unpack why and how those influences are affecting the lived experiences of the learners in the school. This brings us to Team Development Activity B.

Team Development Activity B: Understanding your school's pedagogical beliefs

Purpose: To identify your organisation's Pedagogical Beliefs and how they affect the use of digital technology to support learning.
Time needed: 1 hour

- Step 1: Identifying organisational Pedagogical Beliefs
- Step 2: Reflecting on School Arena Alignment
- Step 3: Reflecting on Classroom Arena Alignment
- Step 4: Reflection on alignment between the school and individual staff

We strongly recommend you use the editable version of this Guided Activity, which you can download from www.onelifelearning.co.uk/resources

Step 1: Identifying organisational pedagogical beliefs

The first part of this activity encourages you to work as a team to identify the Pedagogical Beliefs that are embedded within your School Arena, for example, policies, budgetary decisions, staffing, resources and equipment, strategies, expectations, and 'school norms'.

This activity is best carried out in small groups in order to encourage active discussion and where at least two people in each group have an understanding of pedagogy (e.g. distribute teaching staff, IT staff, and leadership across groups rather than grouping by role).

This activity invites colleagues to reflect on the Influences identified in Team Development Activity A (where you created a display of sticky notes). For each Influence (sticky note), colleagues are asked to identify the Pedagogical Beliefs associated with it. In other words, thinking about what each thing infers about the following:

- views of learners and learning
- views of teachers and teaching
- views of knowledge
- the purpose of schooling

You may find it helpful to return to Table 6.1 (with its descriptors of different aspects of the four main pedagogical stances) or Table 7.2 (with its descriptors of how different technologies can be used differently by those with different Pedagogical Beliefs). The descriptors in both of those tables will help you identify the Pedagogical Beliefs that affect the use of digital technology at your school.

The aim is for colleagues to identify how the Pedagogical Beliefs underpinning each influence (and any associated decisions, policies, norms, routines, or expectations) encourage practice aligned with a particular Pedagogical Stance.

As part of this process, you are likely to discover some inconsistencies. For example, an online behaviour policy may align with a Traditional Pedagogical Stance, whereas a curriculum policy may align with an Individual Constructivist Pedagogical Stance. Or the expectations in two different subject departments may align with two different sets of Pedagogical Beliefs. This is not unusual.

Worked Examples - to help you get started

Take colleagues through this worked example which illustrates how the presence of a trolley of laptops can be shaped by very different Pedagogical Beliefs.

The **influence** of having a trolley of laptops	Chalk Ridge School identified that one of the influences on their current use of digital technology was the presence of a trolley of laptops for each year group. Senior Leaders had decided to fund this purchase and maintenance of those laptops in order that **lessons could incorporate** digital technology.	Mount View School identified that one of the influences on their current use of digital technology was the presence of a trolley of laptops in each year group. Senior leaders had decided to fund the purchase and maintenance of those laptops so that **learners had access** to digital technology during their lessons.

So far, the two schools appear to share exactly the same influence. But look again.

Different **Pedagogical intentions** of having a trolley of laptops	The Pedagogical Intention of the senior leadership team at Chalk Ridge School was about **teacher-led lessons incorporating digital technology**. Teachers were encouraged to look for opportunities to use the laptops where they felt that students' learning would be enhanced. The teachers were thus the gatekeepers of laptop use. **The Pedagogical Intention was framed around the teachers.**	The intention of the senior leadership team at Mount View School was about **learners having access to digital technology** during their lessons. The expectation was that learners would be able to access, choose and use a laptop as and when they felt it would help their given learning activity. The learners were expected to be agentive. **The Pedagogical Intention was framed around the learners.**

The Pedagogical Intentions will create different expectations for how digital technology will be used in the classroom:

Different **Pedagogical Intentions**	At Chalk Ridge School, the Pedagogical Intention means that laptops are likely to be timetabled or planned in advance and incorporated into lesson plans. It is also likely that the laptops will be used for predetermined activities as defined by the teacher with most learners using the same tool or website.	At Mount View School, the Pedagogical Intention means that uses of the laptops are likely to be ad hoc and responsive to learners' ideas about how to complete activities. It is also likely that the laptops will be shared between learners (to encourage dialogue) and used for a range of purposes with learners using different kinds of tools or features.

These different Pedagogical Intentions suggest different underlying Pedagogical Beliefs:

Different **Pedagogical Beliefs**	Teachers are the holders of knowledge. Their role is to instruct the learners. (Traditional stance)	The purpose of school is to support learners in becoming competent in valued ways of working in particular communities. Learners are seen as active and agentive. (Sociocultural stance)

You will note that the language around the likely uses is deliberately tentative. This is because the Pedagogical Intentions *suggest* but will not necessarily *define* practice.

Notes as you start this activity

You will probably find that each Influence affecting the way your school uses digital technology (from Team Development Activity A) becomes a catalyst for discussion about the following:

- What is used
- Who uses it
- How it is used
- Why it is used
- What happens as a result of its use

The easiest way to capture your findings might be to annotate the sticky notes that you used for Activity A with a different coloured pen or use another colour sticky note to stick onto the original set. (You could also use a digital equivalent.)

Your annotation/additional sticky note should state the Pedagogical Stance that seems to be associated with each individual influence (i.e. Traditional, Individual Constructivist, Social Constructivist, Sociocultural). It is particularly helpful if you can choose one colour for each of the Pedagogical Stances (e.g. if the Pedagogical Intention aligned with a Social Constructivist descriptor write in purple, if the Pedagogical Intention aligned with a Traditional stance, write in green, etc.). This will give you an 'at a glance' view of the extent of pedagogical alignment across different influences.

You will find misalignment. Some of this you probably can't do anything about – for example, influences within the Broader context beyond the school. So focus on the things you can do something about – the influences in the School Arena and Classroom Arena.

Step 2: Reflecting on school arena alignment

Within the School Arena, misalignment often occurs between the Pedagogical Stances underpinning:

- the Teaching and Learning policy
- the Behaviour and eSafety policy
- Curriculum design and delivery expectations

Consider the extent to which the Pedagogical Stances embedded within **School Arena** influences align with each other.

If there is misalignment, then the school leadership team should decide on the best strategy for making decisions about what to change in order to enhance internal consistency and how to go about that process. This process of identifying misalignment is the first step in addressing this issue.

Step 3: Reflecting on classroom arena alignment

Consider the extent to which the Pedagogical Stances embedded within **Classroom Arena** influences align with each other.

This is probably best discussed as year or subject teams.

If there is misalignment then the middle leadership team (e.g. subject or year group leaders) should decide, in conjunction with the school senior leadership team, how to address it.

Step 4: Reflection on alignment between the school and individual staff

In order to do this activity, individual staff need to have identified their own personal Pedagogical Beliefs (see Activity 7.2).

Each member of staff should compare their personal Pedagogical Stance (from Activity 7.2 Step 5) with those of the school (from Team Development Activity B Step 1) – focus on the influences that relate to your own practice.

To what extent are the school's Pedagogical Stances aligned with your own personal Pedagogical Beliefs?

It is likely that there will be differences – this is normal, and it is a reflection that we are all human beings with nuanced values and beliefs (see Chapter 5 – The Funnels of Influence).

The focal point should be to look for any groups or trends of Pedagogical Stances that dominate the school context, and how these align (or not) with the Pedagogical Stances of individual staff.

What does this process highlight to you as a team about the need to focus attention on individual or organisational changes?

The elephant in the room

When we introduced the Funnels of Influence in Chapter 5, we highlighted the way that our Substantial Self interprets the Context, creating a Situational Funnel. Within that Situational Funnel, we have an Identity that is specific to that Moment and we perceive there to be a set of expectations relating to that Identity. This means that we are sometimes in a situation in which we feel obliged to meet particular expectations even if we consciously know that they do not align with our personal beliefs. In this scenario, our Situational Identity is prioritising other influences. For example, prioritising the influence of accountability (because of the implications on maintaining paid employment) over social justice (which may be perceived as applying to those other than ourselves).

The pedagogical implications of these compromises are that we 'borrow' pedagogical approaches. For example, a teacher who leads a sociocultural learning environment may recognise that alongside their problem-based learning projects the learners also have to engage with the core curriculum. They may therefore arrange for learners to work individually using adaptive software that introduces the curriculum materials and then tests learners' understanding of it. The learners then move at their own pace through the materials and at times that suit them, with the teacher monitoring progress and providing feedback and support where appropriate. Whilst this does not align with the teacher's Pedagogical Beliefs it is a pragmatic solution to the requirement that learners engage with the core curriculum.

Borrowing pedagogical approaches as a pragmatic solution to a particular situation is not wrong, but it does create conflicting messages for our learners. The mitigation for this is to consider how the borrowed approach is framed to the learners such that it is explained in the context of your wider belief system and the pragmatic constraints within which you have to operate. For example, teachers sometimes use strategies or processes that they do not believe are the most educationally effective, in order for either the teacher or the learner to conform to expectations (e.g. passing tests to achieve qualifications).

Conclusion

Becoming aware of the alignment or lack of alignment between Pedagogical Beliefs, Pedagogical Intentions, and Pedagogical Practices both individually, as well as across an organisation is important. It is likely to be a catalyst for many ongoing conversations between colleagues. This is to be encouraged – because making these embedded Pedagogical Beliefs explicit brings both awareness and clarity about what may need to be refined, reshaped, or reconsidered in order to improve future practice. Those fresh perspectives and insights will translate into greater precision when you plan for your learners both today and in the future.

References

Bandler, R. (2013) *The Ultimate Introduction to NLP: How To Build A Successful Life: The Secret to Living Life*. London: Harper Collins.

Bernstein, B. (1971) *Class, Codes and Control: Theoretical Studies towards a Sociology of Language*. London: Routledge & Kegan Paul.

Burns, M., and Griffith, A., (2018) *The Learning Imperative*. Carmarthen: Crown House.

Cordingley, P., Higgins, S., Greany, T., Buckler, N., Coles-Jordan, D., Crisp, B., Saunders, L., and Coe, R. (2015) *Developing Great Teaching*. London: Teacher Development Trust.

Fletcher-Wood, H. (2018) *Responsive Teaching: Cognitive Science and Formative Assessment in Practice*. London: Routledge.

Fullan, M. (2020) *Leading in a Culture of Change*. London: Jossey Bass.

Fullan, M., Quinn, J., and McEachen, J. (2018) *Deep Learning*. London: SAGE Publications.

Hamachek, D. (1999) 'Effective Teachers: What They Do, How They Do It, and the Importance of Self-Knowledge', in Lipka Richard, P. and Brinthaupt Thomas, M. (eds.) *The Role of Self in Teacher Development*. New York: State University of New York Press.

Hargreaves, A. (2000) 'Four Ages of Professionalism and Professional Learning', *Teachers and Teaching*, 6(2), pp. 151–182.

Hargreaves, A., and O'Connor, M. T. (2018) *Collaborative Professionalism: When Teaching Together Means Learning for All*. London: Sage Publications.

Hattie, J., (2014) *Visible Learning and the Science of How We Learn*. London: Routledge.

Hattie, J. (2018) *Collective Teacher Efficacy*. https://visible-learning.org/2018/03/collective-teacher-efficacy-hattie/

Hattie, J., and Smith, R. (2022) *10 Mindframes for Leaders*. London: SAGE Publications.

Hodges, A. (2015) 'Intertextuality in Discourse', in Tannen, D., Hamilton, H. E., and Schiffrin, D. (eds.) *The Handbook of Discourse Analysis*. 2nd edn. US: Wiley-Blackwell.

Hoogsteen, T. J. (2020) 'Collective Efficacy: Toward a New Narrative of its Development and Role in Achievement'. *Palgrave Commun*, 6(2), pp. 1–7.

Lemov, D. (2021) *Teach Like a Champion 3.0: 63 Techniques that Put Students on the Path to College*. New Jersey: Jossey Bass.

Nelson, T. E., Oxley, Z. M., and Clawson, R. A. (1997) 'Toward a Psychology of Framing Effects', *Political Behavior*, 19(3), pp. 221–246.

Priestley, M., Biesta, G., and Robinson, S. (2015) *Teacher Agency: An Ecological Approach*. London: Bloomsbury.

Salhberg, P. (2015) *Finnish Schools and the Global Education Reform Movement*. London: Routledge.

Sharples, M. (2019) *Practical Pedagogy: 40 New Ways to Teach and Learn*. London: Routledge.

Sherrington, T., and Caviglioli, O. (2020) *Teaching WalkThrus: Five-step Guides for Instructional Coaching*. London: John Catt.

Sims, S., Fletcher-Wood, H., O'Mara-Eves, A., Cottingham, S., Stansfield, C., Van Herwegen, J., and Anders, J. (2021) *What are the Characteristics of Effective Teacher Development? A Systematic Review and Meta Analysis*. London: Education Endowment Foundation.

Tannen, D., Hamilton, H. E., and Schiffrin, D. (eds.) (2015) *The Handbook of Discourse Analysis*. 2nd edn. US: Wiley-Blackwell.

Timperley, H., Wilson, A., Barrar, H., and Fung, I. (2007) *Teacher Professional Learning and Development. Best Evidence Synthesis Iteration (BES)*. Wellington, New Zealand: Ministry of Education.

TPEA (2022) *Intentions v Reality: What's Really Going on for Our Learners When We Use EdTech?*. London: TPEA.

Twining, P., and Aubrey-Smith, F. (2021) "*Trust and Empowerment of Teachers*". The halfbaked.education blog. 31 August 2021. https://halfbaked.education/trust-and-empowerment-of-teachers/

Walker, M. A., Joshi, A. K., and Prince, E. F. (eds.) (1998) *Centering Theory in Discourse*. Oxford: Clarendon Press.

William, D. (2017) *Embedded Formative Assessment: (Strategies for Classroom Assessment That Drives Student Engagement and Learning)*. Bloomington: Solution Tree.

Willingham, D. (2021) *Why Don't Students Like School?: A Cognitive Scientist Answers Questions About How the Mind Works and What It Means for the Classroom*. 2nd edn. NJ: Jossey Bass.

Wilson, J. (1990) *Politically Speaking: The Pragmatic Analysis of Political Language*. Oxford: Basil Blackwell.

CHAPTER

9

Leading precision planning and identifying impact

This chapter takes you through the process of thinking about how to more precisely plan your future uses of digital technology to support learning. However, this chapter is not a guide to curriculum or lesson planning, nor does it set out what an ideal activity or learning experience should look like – each of these will look different depending on your Pedagogical Beliefs and the needs of your learners. As set out at the beginning of this book, our aim is not to promote a particular pedagogical stance but to provoke your thinking. We are aiming to provide prompts which encourage more forensic thinking about your Pedagogical Beliefs and the extent to which they align with your Pedagogical Intentions and Practice.

However, before we continue, it is important to remember that every single decision in a school is ultimately a pedagogical decision. The decisions that we make define the choices that learners can make – choices that will impact their learning. It is important that this is known by every single member of staff, as well as school governors, trustees, board members, and suppliers. The decisions that each person makes in relation to your school will impact the choices that others within the school are consequently able to make. Some decisions may open up Opportunities, and some decisions may reduce Opportunities (think back to the Funnels of Influence in Chapter 5). Every person making decisions – whether small or large in scale – needs to be aware of the consequences and implications of those decisions. The best way to do this is through explicit and regular dialogue – in this case, about Pedagogical Beliefs and how these relate to Pedagogical Practice.

Defining precision planning

As teachers, we use the word *planning* to refer to a range of actions and documents which are created and utilised to inform our classroom actions. Most of these materials refer to Pedagogical Intentions and Pedagogical Approaches even if we don't label them explicitly using those terms. Very few planning materials refer

DOI: 10.4324/9781003321637-9

to Pedagogical Beliefs. We often go into great detail about what we are going to do, how we are going to do it, and what resources, strategies, or techniques we will utilise. We often think about *why* in terms of learning outcomes, but we very rarely identify *why* in terms of our Pedagogical Beliefs.

Precision Planning is about starting with our Pedagogical Beliefs – *why* whatever we are planning is the most effective way to support our learners. Understanding why we are doing something brings greater sense of purpose and greater clarity about actions and shows those around us how much they matter to us (Sinek, Mead, & Docker, 2017; Sinek, 2011). Understanding why we do something is a core feature of being a professional (Hargreaves, 2000). In an educational context, our Pedagogical Beliefs are our *why*.

Precision Planning is also about being better prepared for what Luft and Ingham (1955) refer to as the Johari Window – the different combinations of what we know and our blind spots in any given moment. Precision Planning means understanding our Pedagogical Beliefs and Intentions with enough clarity that when we are in the Moment of Practice and faced with real-time decisions, we know straight away what will create the greatest pedagogical alignment (Chapter 6) and, thus, the greatest consistency and positive impact on our learners' experiences. Fullan and Gallagher (2020) tell us that it is precision which fundamentally underpins improvements in practice because precision requires us to continuously refine our thinking. With Precision Planning, we are preparing our minds as well as our logistics – continuously circling back to our Pedagogical Beliefs and ensuring that they are deeply embedded in everything that we do.

Let's have a look at a practical example that illustrates the need for precision in how we talk about our Pedagogical Intentions. The example which follows is a common pedagogical approach – where a teacher will set a task which is then undertaken by a group of learners utilising digital technology. Teachers often refer to this as collaborative work or group work. Different teachers, with different views on pedagogy, will have different views about what learners working together means in practice. For example,

Pedagogical Stance	**Working together may be interpreted as ...**	**An example of what this looks like when using digital technology**
Traditional	Completing the same task individually, in parallel with each other, whilst seated in a group	A group is assigned the same online worksheet. Learners sit together and complete the task independently, at the same time, each with their own version.
Individual Constructivism	A group of learners completing the same task, with a sub-section assigned to each learner	A group is provided with a shared online document. Each learner completes their own section but has visibility on the whole document.

Social Constructivism	Completing the same task, with every learner actively contributing to the discussion about each part of it	A group creates a shared online concept map. Learners discuss what the key components are and co-author the content.
Sociocultural	Connecting meaningfully with people who have a shared interest in a particular issue or activity	Identifying an expert and arranging a video call to discuss an issue, which then becomes the start of an online group project with a tangible impact beyond the classroom.

Notice how the nature of the interaction between learners differs with each view of pedagogy. In some cases, the activity could not take place without social interaction (e.g. Social Constructivism or Sociocultural). In other cases, the activity could be completed just as easily in complete isolation (e.g. Traditional or Individual Constructivism). Yet, each of the previous activities has been observed in action within the same school, with each teacher referring to the activities as group work.

The reason for highlighting this example is because when using digital technology, teachers often focus on the technology involved or the outcomes achieved through its use (e.g. shared document), rather than considering the holistic experience that the learner will have (e.g. individual contribution).

This lack of consistency leads to confusion for the learner. They become unclear about whether working with others matters or not, and they receive mixed messages from us about how others may or may not play an important role in their future learning.

Before you start using any kind of digital technology (or indeed any kind of resource or tool – including pen and paper), you need to have a clear understanding of how it will support the learning in your classroom. The sequencing of this thinking is important because it must be the pedagogical belief that is considered first – What do you think knowledge is? How do you think people learn? What do you see the role of the teacher as being? Only when you are clear about those sorts of questions should you begin to consider whether and/or how using digital technology (or other resources) might be the best way to help you to achieve the desired learning outcomes.

Precision Planning is therefore about following just three simple steps. As we think about a lesson or activity, we just need to ask ourselves:

1) **What exactly do I want my learners to learn (in light of my beliefs about the purposes of schooling and my view of knowledge)?**
   What is your Pedagogical Stance? (See Guided Activity 7.2, Step 5.)
2) **How do I believe that learners learn?**
   What is the most effective way for me to enhance their learning?

3) **What does evidence suggest the most appropriate pedagogical approaches would be in this context?**
   (See Chapter 2.)
4) **How can I bring greater alignment between my Pedagogical Beliefs, my Pedagogical Intentions, and my Pedagogical Practices?**
   Think about the dimensions of pedagogy (see Table 6.2):
   a) The purpose of education
   b) Views of learners and learning
   c) Views of teachers and teaching
   d) Views of knowledge

Remember that subtle changes can make a significant difference.

Identifying impact

When we set out a definition of Precision Planning at the beginning of this chapter, we encouraged you to think about surfacing your Pedagogical Beliefs in order to bring clarity to decision-making during everyday practice. Ultimately, the aim is to maximise our (positive) impact on our learners' learning.

Internalisations about what it means to be a learner and to learn are not short-term outcomes that evolve from the implementation of a particular Pedagogical Practice but, as discussed in earlier chapters, largely shaped by childhood teachers (Chang-Kredl & Kingsley, 2014). In other words, one of the more significant impacts of your classroom practice is that it is shaping your learners' conceptualisations about what it means to be a learner and to learn, their views on knowledge and the role of school, and their views on what it means to be a teacher and to teach. These ideas are not 'taught' but emerge as a result of subliminal messages that we are giving our learners through every interaction that we have with and around them - all of which are illustrations of our personal Pedagogical Beliefs.

You will have a positive impact if

1) **You are absolutely clear about your own Pedagogical Beliefs** – and develop a healthy habit of active and purposeful discussion about Pedagogical Beliefs with colleagues to ensure continuous reflection and refinement across your team.
2) **You ensure that your Pedagogical Intentions and Practice have integrity because they reflect**
   a) your Pedagogical Beliefs,
   b) evidence from context-relevant and robust research findings about how using digital technology can enhance learning – and any potential unintended consequences (See Chapter 2), and
   c) detailed knowledge of your specific learners' needs and aspirations.

Guided Activity 9.1 provides a framework for evaluating the impact of engaging with the ideas within this book.

Guided Activity 9.1: Exploring impact

You may already be familiar with the work of Guskey (2000), who developed a five-level model to support the evaluation of professional learning – building on the earlier work of Kirkpatrick (1959). Guskey's five-level model has gained academic and school leadership traction because of its accessible approach to connecting theory and practice. Significantly, Guskey sets out the importance of being clear about intended outcomes right from the point of planning.

This activity sets out five potential levels of impact that your engaging with this book may have had, based on Guskey's five levels for evaluating professional learning. Respond to each set of prompts in the right-hand column.

We strongly recommend you use the editable version of this Guided Activity, which you can download from www.onelifelearning.co.uk/resources.

Level 1: **How did you react as you read the book?** (e.g. Did you enjoy it? Did it make you think in greater depth?)	
Level 2: **What have you learnt as you read the book and engaged with the activities?** (Has your thinking changed? If so, how?)	
Level 3: **Has engagement with the book had any impact on your organisation?** (If so, what has changed?)	

Level 4: **Have you made use of what you have learnt in your practice?** (If so, what have you done, what has changed, how, and why?)	
Level 5: **Has engaging with the book had any impact on your learners?** (If so, what, and how do you know?)	

Next steps

As you worked through this book, you have taken a journey through a great many ideas. We have explored complex academic theories, worked through some challenging conceptual ideas, helped you unpack your personal beliefs and practices, and provided recommendations to help you think about your future practice.

The most important conclusion to this book is not the one that we might write as the authors but the conclusion that you leave with as the reader.

This final guided activity therefore invites you to convert the time that you have spent reading this book into practical actions which will have a positive impact on your future professional practice and, most important, on your learners.

Guided Activity 9.2: What will you do next?

When you began to read this book, you had a reason and purpose for doing so. Your journey through this book will be unique to you and will form only part of a wider sequence of thinking that you have around pedagogy and digital technology. We therefore encourage you to take this opportunity to make a concrete action plan about how you will develop your thinking and actions further. As Doran (1981) sets out, this kind of timely, specific, and actionable planning is more likely to lead to future action and impact.

We strongly recommend you use the editable version of this Guided Activity, which you can download from www.onelifelearning.co.uk/resources

Specific What is your target/ goal?	**Measurable** **What impact will this have?** How will you know if you have achieved it?	**Achievable** Realistically what are you going to do?	**Relevant** How will this enhance my pedagogical alignment and improve my learners' learning?	**Time-Bound** When will you do it? When will it be completed?

Conclusion

Our aim in writing this book has been to encourage greater precision in the way that we all think and talk about the use of digital technology to support learning.

In taking you on a journey through this book, we hope that you will have engaged in the opportunities to reflect and probe into your own thinking, beliefs, intentions, and practices. Whatever those beliefs are, we hope that you finish this book with a more precise and detailed understanding of them, how they were formed, how they impact your practice today, and how you might refine your future practice further as a result of this more forensic understanding.

The Digital Divide is no longer just about access to devices and connectivity. As increasingly argued by many worldwide, the Digital Divide is now magnified by the choices that we make in our classrooms (Aubrey-Smith & Yusuf, 2022; OUP, 2021).

There are learners all around the world who are already benefiting from the opportunities that become possible through precision in our thinking about our Pedagogical Beliefs. This will, in turn, support clearly conceptualised, purposeful, and precise uses of digital technology.

The most powerful thing that you can do as an educator is to be absolutely, forensically clear about what your Pedagogical Beliefs are, and how you will ensure precise alignment between those beliefs, your intentions, and your practices in future.

If we are not able (or willing) to align our Pedagogical Beliefs and Practices or to meaningfully utilise digital technology to support learning effectively, then are we – perhaps inadvertently – magnifying inequalities?

What kind of future do you really want to create for your learners?

Making that kind of future a reality depends entirely on what you choose to do next.

References

Aubrey-Smith, F., and Yusuf, B. (2022) 'Closing the Digital Divide: What Can Schools Do?', *Headteacher Update*. 27 September 2022.

Chang-Kredl, S., and Kingsley, S. (2014) 'Identity Expectations in Early Childhood Teacher Education: Pre-service Teachers' Memories of Prior Experiences and Reasons for Entry into the Profession', *Teaching and Teacher Education*, 43, pp. 27–36.

Doran, G. T. (1981). 'There's a S.M.A.R.T. Way to Write Management's Goals and Objectives', *Management Review*, 70(11), pp. 35–36.

Fullan, M., and Gallagher, M. (2020) *The Devil is in the Details: System Solutions for Equity, Excellence and Student Well-Being*. London: Corwin.

Guskey, T. R. (2000) *Evaluating Professional Development*. California: Corwin Press.

Hargreaves, A. (2000) 'Four Ages of Professionalism and Professional Learning', *Teachers and Teaching: History and Practice*, 6(2), pp. 151–182.

Kirkpatrick, D. L. (1959) 'Techniques for Evaluation Training Programs', *Journal of the American Society of Training Directors*, 13, pp. 21–26.

Luft, J., and Ingham, H. (1955) 'The Johari Window, A Graphic Model of Interpersonal Awareness'. *Proceedings of the Western Training Laboratory in Group Development.* Los Angeles: University of California.

Oxford University Press (2021) *Addressing the Deepening Digital Divide.* Oxford: OUP.

Sinek, S. (2011) *Start With Why: How Great Leaders Inspire Everyone to Take Action.* London: Penguin.

Sinek, S., Mead, D., and Docker, P. (2017) *Find Your Why: A Practical Guide for Discovering Purpose for You and Your Team.* London: Penguin.

Index